America's 18 Hour Work Week

OR

Where Have All The Profits Gone?

by

Robert A. Nass

Published by

R & E PUBLISHERS
P. O. Box 2008
Saratoga, California 95070

Artwork by
MARY ANN MONTGOMERY

Typesetting by
ESTELLA M. KREBS

Library of Congress Card Catalog Number
86-60822

I.S.B.N.
0-88247-755-2

DEDICATION

This book is dedicated to

. . . my wife, Yvonne, for her love, support
and patience

. . . our 7 children — Bob, Curt, Paula, Jeff,
Scott, Tracy and Chris

. . .my mother, Helen Halvorsen Schuelie

TABLE OF CONTENTS

"REPAIRS AND MAINTENANCE" — A Comprehensive Program

INTRODUCTION

Business and industry spend millions of dollars annually in attempts to reduce financial losses caused by on-the-job accidents, mistakes, absenteeism, preoccupation, impulsive behavior and sabotage.

No business or industry is immune to the problem. In management's efforts to curb and reduce such losses, various experimental methods have been tried. Few have produced more than minor success.

Effective solutions remain elusive because the real problem has not been traced to its origins — lack of understanding of human behavior. When on-the-job behavior is correctly understood, it can be influenced and day-to-day losses attributable to that behavior can be dramatically curtailed.

Getting to the root of people-problems requires that both management and labor make a serious, thorough evaluation of their individual and collective behavior.

"*How* can this be fixed?" is the wrong question.

The right question is, "*Why* does this happen?"

After determining what makes people behave the way they do, effective measures can be taken to change counterproductive behavior.

The "WORK" Side
Of The Bridge

- From Twig to Tree
- Bridge to the Marketplace
- The Iceberg Syndrome
- The "Personal Business" Factor

FROM TWIG TO TREE:
DISRESPECT FOR CHILDREN

Business and industry's problems with low productivity begin in the cradle.

Historically, children have been treated as though they were without feelings. They have been ignored, insulted, rejected, belittled, misused and abused. Throughout history there has been a lack of respect for children.

This is not surprising since only one hundred years ago it was not uncommon for a father to sell one or more of his children. There are still isolated cases in which this is done but fortunately it is no longer common.

The first child abuse case occurred in New York City about one hundred years ago and was won by the Society for the Prevention of Cruelty to Animals (SPCA). At that time, there were no laws or organizations protecting the rights of children. The SPCA argued effectively that humans were animals and the abused child was entitled to the agency's protection.

Even the child labor law, enacted in 1938, was not completely altruistic. This law was enacted during the Great Depression when there was high unemployment. Jobs were scarce and children were removed from the workforce for reasons that had little to do with their welfare. Adults needed and demanded those jobs.

Today, child abuse falls into five categories:

- physical abuse, better known as the "battered child syndrome"
- physical neglect, the failure to provide a child with adequate diet, shelter, clothing and other physical care
- sexual abuse, including intimidating glances and remarks as well as engaging a child in sexual acts
- verbal abuse, demeaning remarks such as "You're dumb" or "You never do anything right" or "Nobody loves you"
- emotional neglect, resulting from unmet needs for love, support, time and attention.

When children are abused or feel demeaned, neglected or rejected, they will silently consider their options. Being unsophisticated in communication skills, they act out options behaviorally. The options will included excessive or exaggerated need for *attention*; an attempt to gain *power and control*; or surprisingly calculated *sabotage*.

Attention

The need for attention can be acted out in various ways. Children may adopt the "clinging vine" approach, insisting upon being physically close to one or both parents, shadowing every move, always underfoot. Or they may force communication and verbal involvement by asking endless questions, not for information, but to keep the parent engaged. They may exhibit exaggerated jealousy when asked to share the parents' time with others. These strategies produce unfavorable rather than favorable reaction from parents and other adults.

Being accident prone is a very effective ploy that works well, at least initially. The accidents need not be serious, just enough to require assistance. At first, parents and siblings run to the aid of the injured. The "cry wolf" syndrome is soon discovered and future re-

4

sponses from parents are usually casual and the behavior is discouraged. The child may stumble down a few steps, scream and feign injury and the parent snaps, "Oh, stop being silly." The parent is insensitve to the underlying causes of such behavior. The child cannot verbally explain emotional pain and so continues to struggle for recognition and acceptance.

The "class clown" illustrates how well silliness attracts attention. Helplessness also is a technique used successfully even by very small children and they become quite adept at coercing others to do things for them. Still other children may opt for daredevil behavior, taking dangerous chances and calculated risks to draw attention to themselves, or fighting in the schoolyard to gain the center-ring spotlight.

The reason — they feel ignored and neglected.

The goal — to feel important and accepted.

Unfortunately, these types of behavior eventually become ineffective because people soon learn the game and refuse to be a part of it. Most people do not understand the real underlying reasons for the game—the child, even older children, cannot convey the real reasons and the underlying problem.

When these types of behavior become unsuccessful, children progress to their next option.

Power and Control

A child's goal is always to achieve a feeling of importance, acceptance, usefulness and love. When they realize that their ploys for attracting attention are failing, they may try to gain power and control over the parents or other authority figures such as teachers by attempting to force them to devote more of their time or attention to them or by displaying a sign of power. Power struggles provoke anger. Anger creates emotional distance and a deeper wedge further splits the relationship between parent and child. This reaction, in turn, raises the child's anxiety level and creates an even greater need for power. The vicious, negative cycle continues.

The child's goal of achieving importance, acceptance, usefulness and love is compounded with a new goal — thwart the will of the parent. This gives the child a sense of importance and power.

Exhibited in very early childhood, the behavior can manifest itself as a refusal to be dressed. At first, the parent may playfully treat the resistance as a game but with increasing frustration, anger, and sometimes, rage becoming the dominant emotions.

Later on, the same child may decide at the last minute not to join a preplanned family outing. The "stubborn as a mule" strategy is being tried.

During childhood, and continuing through late adolescence, "contrary" behavior continues in the child's reluctance to do assigned chores or to give minimal effort to avoid severe punishment.

A father may ask for some newspaper to start a fire in the outdoor fireplace. The child brings back a single half-sheet.

A child usually acquiesces but only after extensive pleading, coaxing and threats, further frustrating and angering the parent. The child's behavior was purposeful and successful. As children begin to realize the effect of their power, they become more skillful at wielding it.

Arguing with direction is a useful weapon for the child. Usually they disagree with instructions and then observe as the parent is provoked into a full-blown argument. The parent rarely realizes that this situation is an "explanation" of the child's desperate need for power and control in the environment.

This difficult and frustrating behavior is what psychiatrists call passive-aggressive; difficult and frustrating because a child either agrees to complete a task and then fails to do so or does it so slowly that the process causes the parent intense irritation.

To further illustrate, a youngster agrees to take out the trash and then asks the parent, "Can I get you a cup of coffee first?" The parent welcomes such thoughtfulness and thoroughly enjoys the coffee. Nice kid! An hour later the parent realizes that the trash is still in the kitchen and the battle begins.

It is the youngster's way of expressing anger. Such children are trying to say that they don't like the way they are being treated. They don't feel strong enough or confident enough or safe enough to deal with the parent directly and confrontationally. They desperately need to be acknowledged, listened to, accepted and taken seriously. When the effort toward acceptance fails, their next option is sabotage.

Sabotage

This behavior can be adopted by a child at a very early age. It embraces the universal philosophy, "Defeat the enemy even if it means self-destruction." Most adults are incapable of helping children at this stage because they fail to realize that when children have exhausted so many previous options, they will unwittingly adopt a destructive attitude. The child then resembles the young officer in Viet Nam who ordered an artillery strike against his own position in order to stop the enemy advancement.

The only "artillery" at a child's disposal is the power of skillful sabotage and one of the most effective weapons in the arsenal is the power to "strike." School performance is the ideal place to initiate the shutdown.

Given the value which our society places on education, children realize that few things will hurt and worry parents more than a decline in grades. It assures immediate attention. The parent is not likely to understand the underlying reason for suddenly poor grades and so they react to the child's school performance rather than the child's real problem.

Being generally disruptive is another way in which a child can sabotage. In an academic setting, this behavior can result in a parent-teacher conference which might also include a school counselor and someone in charge of discipline. In this type of situation, the child is usually quiet. Silently relishing the scene they have orchestrated, the

7

children congratulate themselves on a job well done; destructive but effective. They certainly do have everyone's attention.

Carelessness and sarcasm are further, albeit softer, signs of disruption but the more desperate children will consider a final, two-pronged option. Unconsciously, their actions will result either in a brush with the law or in withdrawal. They can steal, damage or destroy property, or make other choices from a long list of viable options. Or their discouragement may slip into silence. In either case, parents are reduced to the point of frenzied helplessness. The withdrawn child clearly exhibits distress but, refusing to share it with anyone, spends increasing amounts of time alone. The parents cannot understand such behavior and are unable to either motivate or excite the child.

Surprisingly, both the child and the family appear to survive such cataclysmic upheaval. The child grows up and, joining a new generation of employees, "crosses the bridge" to the marketplace.

It is at this juncture that management must examine the wisdom of Alexander Pope: "As the twig is bent, so grows the tree."

THE BRIDGE TO THE MARKETPLACE

The legion of young people eventually reaches employable age. Most have graduated from high school and many from college. They take their "baggage of behavior" and "cross the bridge to the marketplace."

The bridge is the transition from the domestic family environment to the business/industrial environment. Their "baggage" is the need for *attention* and for *power and control*. The baggage includes the techniques used to meet these needs. Only the stage and props have changed; the script is the same.

Instead of poor school grades, there are delayed reports or below-capacity effort. Instead of staring out the window during English class, there is time spent away from the desk or project. The knee skinned in the schoolyard becomes an industrial accident. Behavior doesn't change unless something specific is done to re-direct.

Small problems in the family environment become larger, more serious problems in the business/industrial environment, with the additional dimension of economic consequences. In the marketplace, behavior arising from unsatisfied needs for attention, power and control is costing business and industry billions of dollars every year. To solve problems, it is necessary to first understand them. Observing the terrain on both sides of the bridge, there are striking similarities in need for attention between the young and the not so young.

Attention

The need for attention can be very selective and specific. Characteristic is the person who takes time out to chat informally and at length, any time, with whomever will listen. It can be men who engage women in conversation, or vice versa. It can be an employee who continually engages the boss with suggestions or new ideas. The reverse is also not uncommon. It can be the staffer who always needs help. The need to be noticed is so strong that it dominates work time.

The need for attention is obvious in the office "clowns." They talk too loud. They play schoolboy tricks on co-workers — hiding pens, keys, purses; leaving fake telephone messages; moving desks and chairs; switching nameplates — pranks that may be annoying but don't seem harmful. Viewed as isolated incidents, they usually are not harmful. They can even have a positive effect if they relieve some group tension or lower the stress level.

The effect of office pranks must be gauged by their frequency and the level and extent of harm done. This judgment is similar to that used in determining child abuse. A child who is spanked once a year is not usually thought of as abused. A child severely beaten, even once a year, has been abused. A child who is spanked several times a week also is being abused.

Another manifestation of the need for attention is daredevil behavior. The daredevil takes unnecessary chances or takes risks that prudent adults would not take. The reckless deed is usually done in the presence of others or at least reported to others after the fact. Daredevil behavior should not be confused with taking reasonable risks to achieve valid goals.

Power and Control

The search for power and control is not in itself neurotic or negative. It is, according to some theorists, innate in everyone.

Alfred Adler, a Viennese physician, noted that newborns are utterly helpless. If they are not given water and food, they will die. If they are not protected from harsh environments, they will die. They are totally dependent upon adults for survival. Adler believed that early recognition of this dependency creates anxiety and that all behavior henceforth is aimed at reducing that neonatal anxiety.

A supportive, caring environment enables the child to feel safe, experience love, and develop social skills that build confidence and self-esteem, thus satisfying Maslow's 3rd and 4th (love and self-esteem) levels in the hierarchy of needs.

Achievement of love and self-esteem are thwarted when a child is either neglected or overindulged. The neglected as well as the pampered child develops more anxiety which in turn intensifies the need to acquire power and control in order to relieve the anxiety. This vicious cycle continues to increase anxiety which then produces chronic feelings of discouragement and inferiority. At this point, the techniques used to gain power and control become destructive.

Our need to grow from dependency to self-sustaining independence is normal. The path of "growing up" is from anxious, self-centered, dependent infant to self-confident, independent adult with a healthy self-esteem. If the normal path of adulthood is blocked at early stages by neglect, lack of support and direction, discouragement and frustrated feelings of worthlessness, society and business are later confronted by adults who have the feelings of angry, anxious children, desperate to gain enough power and control over their surroundings to feel "safe."

The adult quest for power and control is the same quest as that of adolescence or childhood; perhaps more sophisticated and skillful because of long years of experience. The tantrums of childhood have become oppositional behavior in the adult.

An employee who challenges authority cannot comfortably deal with the supervisor's orders and directions or with suggestions and advice from coworkers. The rationale is couched in different terms than in earlier years but the motive is the same — to make others back down, to gain control, to be in command. Controlling means being safe (at last) and feeling powerful (at last) rather than worthless and dependent.

Personnel psychologists, managers and supervisors might note that the employee is strongly motivated to achieve. However, the employee's goal is at odds with the goal of good industrial relations. The employee's objective is to gain self-esteem. This is a personal, self-centered objective which is, by its nature, contrary to cooperative endeavor.

If the employee's (or manager's) drive to achieve a sense of importance is thwarted in the workplace (as it has been during childhood and adolescence), there will soon be evidence of disruptive and destructive behavior.

Such child-adult employees are repeatedly late for work, late with reports, late for meetings, late starting or finishing projects. The message is clear. "You can't make me do something I don't want to do. You're not in control. I am."

Perhaps the most difficult behavior to deal with is what psychiatrists call passive-aggressive behavior. It can also be called defiant obedience. Familiar examples:

- Little boy says to his mother in an angry and sarcastic way, "Yes, *Ma'am!*" or a private to the lieutenant, with an abrupt salute, "Yes, *Sir!*" They are really saying, "Go to +*@!*!"
- Mother says to the son, "Why aren't the dishes done?" Response: "There's no dishcloth."
- Supervisor to worker, "Why aren't the reports ready?" Response: "The typewriter needs a new ribbon cartridge and the stockroom hasn't delivered any yet."
- Father to son: "Bring in some firewood." Son comes back with one stick.
- Supervisor: "Get me some more paper for this job." Employee brings a single sheet.

Situations like these are common and happen at all echelons, every shift, every day. These incidents provoke anger. Anger begets anger. Repressed anger causes preoccupation, which leads to mistakes, accidents and thoughts, even plans, of revenge. At home, the cost is constant friction and a fragmented family. In the marketplace, the cost in dollars is astronomical from lost time, productivity and material. An employee's struggle for power and control has failed to get the desired results. The psychological movement of frustrated needs is progressive, from attention to power and control to sabotage.

Sabotage

Sabotage occurs in every company, from minor pilfering to major damage that may cost millions of dollars.

It is done in small retail stores by altering prices, breakage or giving customers more than is required. In larger companies, it is done by allowing faulty work to pass or even causing the product to be faulty − leaving valves open or closed, whichever causes a problem; omitting information that will help another employee; tearing bags causing loss of raw or finished material; introducing foreign matter to chemicals, food, oil.

There was an employee who worked in the canning unit of a large oil company. His job was to keep the empty cans from jamming up on the moving track to the filler spout. When the cans moved smoothly along, he had only to sit and watch the line. He was doing just that one day. Only this time, he had a small pile of pebbles and cinders at hand and as the cans moved past, he dropped a small stone into as many of the cans as the pace of the moving track would allow.

Reason: He had recently lost a grievance to the company. First, his complaint was ignored. Then his attempt to exert pressure and control through the union failed.

Goal: Revenge.

Method: Sabotage.

Sabotage occurs in many forms − slowed production, purposely producing inferior quality, omitting information, damage to equipment, raw material, finished product and to property.

The Attention/Power and Control/Sabotage syndrome operates in all echelons, not only at blue collar levels.

The director of a large corporation held daily staff meetings with his managers. He talked rapidly, announced conclusions without supplying intermediate information or rationale and issued commands with no time for questions and discussion.

Managers left such meetings in confusion, regrouping to confer with each other in an attempt to clarify their orders and proper responsibilities.

The director had the reputation of being sharp-witted and decisive. A closer look reveals a man with a strong need to retain control. Information is omitted or skimmed over on purpose. Retention of key information forces managers to keep coming back to the director for clarification and specificity, enhancing the director's apparent importance.

This level of control is difficult to perceive and almost impossible to challenge. It occurs frequently and the hidden cost is high.

Business and industry can improve employee productivity through reward systems such as Employee Assistance Programs (EAPs) and in-house health spas and stress-relief workshops but until management is better trained to recognize basic human needs and drives, the impact of personal and family problems on efficiency and productivity will continue to be costly.

Domestic and personal problems will continue to cross the bridge into the marketplace, every shift, every day.

THE ICEBERG SYNDROME

In an old Mutt and Jeff cartoon, Mutt is on his hands and knees under the street light. The scene is at night. Jeff asks, "What are you doing?"

"I'm looking for a quarter I lost."

"Where did you lose it?"

"Down the street."

"Then why are you looking here?"

"Because there's more light here."

The same rationale is often used in trying to improve employees' performance. Much time, energy and money is spent looking for an effective solution without realizing where the problem is or how it sustains itself.

Low productivity can't be solved under the street light because its major cause is back there in the dark; in the relative obscurity of human behavior.

One must go where the quarter is in order to recover it.

The place to look for the missing money is among those employees whose day-to-day performance is considered average and, on the whole, acceptable. That is where the most money is being lost.

Investors/shareholders/owners are in business to make a profit on their investment. Salaries are one cost of doing business — so owners understandably want maximum productivity per payroll dollar. Owners hire administrators who can produce that result for them. Administrators use incentives and rewards systems to increase productivity, often with excellent results.

In the days of sweatshops, owners accomplished their objective through fear. Modern management gets better results through motivation.

For at least half a century, management has found that employees motivated toward common company goals will cooperate in a smoothly run operation and do it profitably. Most businesses find this method of management effective most of the time.

Even so, a subtle counterforce continues unchecked that impels all employees sometimes and some employees all of the time toward counterproductive behavior — honest mistakes caused mostly by preoccupation; accidents resulting from carelessness or impulsiveness or daredevil behavior; absenteeism that is largely due to discouraged feelings and apathy. The most extreme form of counterproductive behavior is intentional sabotage.

Every college textbook on personnel psychology or human relations in supervision and management offers at least a chapter on motivation. Most of the early studies and experiments singled out environmental conditions as a motivational factor that needed improvement: lighting, temperature, ventilation and noise levels.

When physical working conditions improved, productivity improved. Management had found a successful "tool." Now color schemes in offices and factories are given serious consideration. Carefully selected, piped-in music is widely used. Each improvement raises productivity a little.

Researchers have also traced low productivity to fatigue and boredom due to monotony. Lost time due to accidents has always held center stage attention. Most companies offer incentives to counteract these problems.

Safety prizes are awarded — the longer the accident-free period, the better the prize.

Employees are encouraged to take an active part in the improvement of the company by submitting suggestions on cost reduction, product improvements, and methods to increase efficiency.

Employee suggestions commonly save the company approximately three times the amount of money paid out in even the largest prize awards.

And still the daily losses to a company or organization from mistakes, absenteeism, accidents and overt or subtle sabotage persist. Ad hoc methods are not achieving the goal of maximum productivity per payroll dollar.

Some incentive approaches don't work at all. Others work well enough to justify their costs and even give a modest but noticeable return.

The Simon Legree school of management is a proven failure. Dictatorial slave-driving and constant threats can be effective temporarily or short-term but such an approach contains the seeds of its own destruction. It breeds rising resentment and is soon undermined by the overt and covert actions of its employee/victims.

On the other hand, the Santa Claus school of management doesn't work either. Some administrators make repeated concessions, hoping that employees will appreciate the generosity of their benefactor and express that appreciation through a maximum effort at the desk or workbench. It sounds reasonable but it doesn't work. People generally become frightened, edgy and disruptive when they don't know where the limits are; and efficiency and productivity go predictably down.

Major sabotage is rarely a problem. What gives management the most intractable difficulty is employees' subtle disregard and disrespect for company product, equipment, time and property and their indifference or tacit antagonism to company goals. It takes supervisory skill to discern, pinpoint and analyze the extent and causes of this kind of silent sabotage.

A farmhand was sent to the orchard to separate and count the good apples. At the end of the day, he had very few apples in his basket. When asked why, he answered, "Counting them is no problem. It's deciding which ones to keep that gives me trouble."

The apple-sorting for supervisors and managers is in deciding which employees contribute how much and how often to shortages in yield, unmet deadlines, flaws or inferiority in the finished product.

Supervisors logically tackle the most conspicuous problem. To reduce accidents, employees are given training in fire and safety procedures. Posters are designed emphasizing safety measures and efficient production.

Wear your safety glasses.
Do it right the first time.

Supervisors attend seminars to learn more effective ways to cope with production problems and labor negotiations.

The last ditch approach, and a costly one, is to do whatever seems most immediately expedient, and add the cost to the price of the finished product.

This makes consumers unhappy. Unhappy consumers are bad for business. Declines in business means layoffs and salary cuts. Nobody wins.

And the beat goes on.

Two popular and successful incentive programs are Employee Assistance Programs (EAPs) and stress management programs.

EAPs are being set up by more and more major companies. Smaller companies band together to split the costs of running an EAP. The 1983-1984 cost was approximately $15 to $16 per employee annually. Some EAPs may cost as much as $20 per employee annually. Even so, many EAPs produce a $3 return in productivity for every $1 invested in the program.

The annual cost of an EAP for a company with 1,000 employees would be approximately $15,000. This amount would cover services including the distribution of educational literature (pamphlets and posters), training for supervisors (often in alcoholism) and 10-12 counseling sessions for employees who either seek counseling or whose job is made contingent upon accepting a term of professional counseling.

The 3-1 return to this company would be $45,000 per year.

An extra $45,000 per year on the profit/loss statement sounds impressive and it is, both in dollar return and the number of employees who may be helped by such a program. Unfortunately, the number of employees helped by such a program is miniscule compared to the total number on the payroll.

A successful EAP projects service-usage at 3% of the total complement of staff. Less than one-third of this 3%, or less than 1%, of all employees will be impaired to the point of being threatened with job loss.

In a company of 1,000 employees, losses through mistakes, accidents, preoccupation, absenteeism and direct sabotage run into the millions. (See Figure 1.) Assuming an annual loss of $5.5 million attributable to these causes, a $45,000 return on a $15,000 investment looks less impressive. Reducing a $5.5 million loss by $45,000 equals less than 1%.

This means that over 97% of the losses sustained stem from the other 97% of company employees who are unaffected by the EAP. This tip-of-the-iceberg approach does little to curtail day-to-day losses.

EAPs are important and effective programs but they must be expanded to reach the unaffected 97%. They must be designed, managed and staffed by personnel who fully understand the impact that angry, frightened and discouraged employees have on daily productivity.

A more recent development in staff assistance is the introduction of programs for "stress management." These have been offered primarily to white collar workers.

The emphasis is on relaxation exercises and improved physical fitness. Many larger companies have hired physical fitness instructors to help and direct employees in the program. In some cases, the program is conducted on company time; in others, it is scheduled by staggered lunch hours. Space and equipment are supplied by the company.

Stress management in the form of relaxation techniques is becoming increasingly popular. These vary from meditation techniques to instructor-led group exercises. The object is to achieve a "tran-state" – a sensation of floating, a state of near total relaxation.

It must be emphasized that these programs and exercises are beneficial and should be continued. It is also important to point out that these too affect only the tip of the iceberg – a small percentage of the employees and a small superficial part of the basic problem.

To reduce and minimize stress in daily life, people need to confront the things that are causing the stress. Individuals can't control their environment or world events, of course, so there will always be some stress in their lives. But individuals can learn to minimize and prevent almost all of the personal conflicts that cause most of the daily stress.

"Stress" is a very imprecise term, a generalization with no specific clues to cause. One might consult a therapist, saying only that there is a problem, without clearly stating what the problem is. It might relieve some anxiety to just admit there is a problem but until the problem is clearly defined and confronted, there will be no significant, lasting change.

The same applies to stress. A half hour of meditation may very well do some good but until the conflict that causes the stress is confronted and options considered, it is doubtful that much will change.

Unfortunately, people will continue, like Mutt in the lamppost scene, to do what is least uncomfortable and threatening for them even though the results are minimal in comparison to the persistent loss in time, energy, and human suffering.

Companies will continue to praise the savings of $45,000 while millions go out the back door.

The symptoms of silent subversion by troubled employees will continue to adversely affect job performance, productivity and profitability: accidents, mistakes, preoccupation, absenteeism, impulsive behavior and sabotage.

THE "PERSONAL BUSINESS" FACTOR

Employees are expensive. Salaries and fringe benefits are often the largest cost item in an organization's budget. Accountants factor this item into the formula for pricing the finished product. There is no problem unless the product is priced out of the competitive market. When this happens, managers take a sharp look at employees' productivity rates to make sure the company is getting a day's work for a day's pay.

A portion of wage costs is routinely wasted, every working day, by employees conducting "personal business" on the job. Some employers may be lenient in their unofficial policy toward such activity. Many employees expect such leniency as a "non-contractual fringe benefit."

Two kinds of "personal business" are common. A few employees deliberately use company time and materials to conduct a sideline business for purely personal profit. This kind of abuse can be corrected by careful supervision and better security measures. Or the company may choose to look the other way for some overriding reason. The solution in these cases is always a management decision.

The other kind of "personal business" is neither so noticeable nor so easy to control or correct because the employees are not *intentionally* cheating the employer. They are physically on the job but their minds are somewhere else, conducting "personal business."

This kind of personal business may be an unhappy marriage, trouble with a child, friction with relatives, some long-suppressed anger or resentment, or corrosively low self-esteem.

Employees at all levels of any organization bring this kind of "personal business" to work with them. Efficiency and productivity go down. Mistakes, oversights and minor injuries go up. Employees' personal and family problems are enormously costly to employers.

Experts in the field of tests and measurements have found that aptitude, personality characteristics, specific kinds of achievement and other performance traits will cluster within a normal range in most situations. Plotting these characteristics and traits on a frequency curve reveals a normal or bell-shaped curve. There is a larger portion clustered around the center, with a normal point. The curve is bilaterally symmetrical, with as many cases above normal as below.

A random sample of a sizeable company will usually show employees' productivity as a bell-shaped or normal curve. On any given day, 2% will present as overachievers, giving 8+ hours to their assigned task. Output will diminish to about 2% who will present as underachievers, giving only 2 or less hours to their assigned task. The average worker will give approximately 5 hours to their assigned task on any given day or shift. (See Figure 1.)

To approximate the cost of nonproductive job time in an organization of 1,000 employees, assume an average cost to the employer of $8.00 per payroll hour. (This figure approximates the 1984 figure of the U. S. Department of Labor, Bureau of Labor Statistics for private, non-agricultural, non-supervisory earnings.) Further assume an average work year to include 230 days. (See Table 1.)

The itemized losses are staggering — and especially since they deal with only *one* behavioral aspect of the troubled employee — preoccupation. Losses through mistakes are not included nor are sabotage, accidents or excessive sick time.

Not many companies can absorb such losses day after day. Good supervisors and managers will seek new skills and resources to deal effectively with discouraged and troubled employees whose job

(Figure 1)

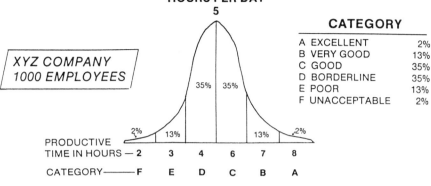

AVERAGE PRODUCTIVE HOURS PER DAY

CATEGORY	
A EXCELLENT	2%
B VERY GOOD	13%
C GOOD	35%
D BORDERLINE	35%
E POOR	13%
F UNACCEPTABLE	2%

XYZ COMPANY
1000 EMPLOYEES

(Table 1)
FORMULA FOR WORK DAYS:

DAYS OF THE YEAR	WEEKENDS	HOLIDAYS	VACATION	SICKDAYS	PERSONAL DAYS	DAYS WORKED ANNUALLY
365	104	8	12	8	3	230

CATEGORY	NO. OF EMPLOYEES	POSSIBLE HRS. PER DAY	HOURS LOST	POSSIBLE TOTAL DAILY PAYROLL	DAILY TOTAL DOLLAR LOSS TO COMPANY
A	20	160	—	$ 1,280	—
B	130	1040	130	8,320	$ 1,040
C	350	2800	700	22,400	5,600
D	350	2800	1400	22,400	11,200
E	130	1040	650	8,320	5,200
F	20	160	120	1,280	960
	1000	8000	3000	$64,000	$24,000

DAILY PAYROLL	**$64,000**
DAILY LOSS	**$24,000**
ANNUAL PAYROLL	**$16,640,000***
ANNUAL LOSS	**$5,520,000****

*Based on potential work days annually.
40 (hours/week) X 52 (weeks) X $8.00 (per hour) X 1000 (employees) = $16,640,000.00

**Based on formula for actual days worked.
230 (average days worked annually) X $24,000.00 (daily loss) = $5,520,000.00

23

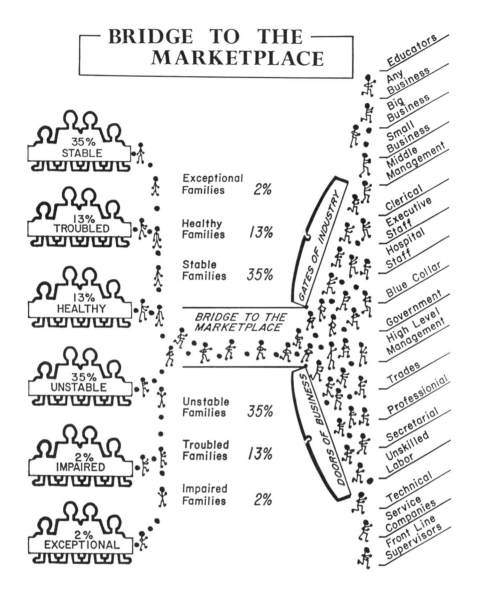

BRIDGE TO THE MARKETPLACE

35% STABLE

13% TROUBLED

13% HEALTHY

35% UNSTABLE

2% IMPAIRED

2% EXCEPTIONAL

Exceptional Families	2%
Healthy Families	13%
Stable Families	35%
Unstable Families	35%
Troubled Families	13%
Impaired Families	2%

BRIDGE TO THE MARKETPLACE

GATES OF INDUSTRY

DOORS OF BUSINESS

Educators
Any Business
Big Business
Small Business
Middle Management
Clerical
Executive Staff
Hospital Staff
Blue Collar
Government
High Level Management
Trades
Professional
Secretarial
Unskilled Labor
Technical
Service Companies
Front Line Supervisors

performance is making such a costly impact on the company.

Most managers would of course like to attain a consistent productivity rate at the levels of Categories A and B. It is unrealistic to think that 100% of the staff will be 100% productive day after day or even on any given day. It is just as unrealistic to believe that the "normal" figures cannot be improved.

The data from Figure 1 shows that 85% of the employees (Categories C, D, E and F) in XYZ Company average 4.62 hours of output. If only Categories D, E and F are considered (i.e., 50% of the company's work force), the average is 3.66 hours of productivity.

Management's failure to improve upon these figures is due to failure to recognize and understand the problem — 85% of their staff is distracted and discouraged; 50% is very upset and a large proportion of that 50% is angry enough to act out their anger in a dramatic way.

Such employees are discouraged, frightened and angry because something is amiss in their personal lives. That discouragement, fear and anger is brought with them through the doors of business and the gates of industry and is acted out in the marketplace.

In this sense, the troubled domestic family becomes the troubled business/industrial family. If the domestic family is the source of the troubled business/industrial family, corporate leaders must find a way to deal with both "families." Treating only part of the problem will produce only part of the solution.

Management's tendency to accept low productivity as normal stems from the cultural attitude that the privacy of family life is sacrosanct and no outsider has a right to intrude or interfere.

Many experts in the field of mental health and the more specialized field of alcoholism are finding that a troubled person is rarely found in an otherwise healthy family. To find a troubled person is to find a troubled family. To find an alcoholic is to find an alcoholic family. This does not mean that everyone in the family is alcoholic but rather that conditions are right for everyone in that family to manifest serious behavior problems.

Capable executives will not find it impossible to make dramatic, and consistent, improvements in productivity rates. Our nation moves large armies to accomplish objectives. We spend billions of dollars to achieve goals in defense, in exploration and in medical research. Corporations spend millions of dollars in advertising and promotion. It is not unreasonable to believe that business and industry can reduce the wasted time factor by at least 50% among the 85% of employees in Categories C, D, E, and F. (See Figure 2.)

Clearly, the most obvious offenders are but the tip of the iceberg and the other 97% of the total wasted-time loss of $5.5 million is not even questioned. Something is terribly wrong. The current approach to business and industry's serious economic problems is, bluntly, "penny wise and pound foolish."

The first corrective step is a new awareness and understanding of the constant interaction of the domestic family with the business/industrial family. Each is subject to the same dynamics as the other.

Families do not like others to intrude into their "private" affairs. If one member of a family is having a problem, the others rally round to help. But the "helping" members, through either ignorance or self-defense, will obdurately refuse to see that the family problem is one to which *all* of them contribute in some major or minor way. Exactly the same dynamic applies in the business/industrial family.

It will require some courage for all employees, from top to bottom, to take a fearless and thorough personal inventory of their own attitudes and behavior — an indepth examination of their own skills, or lack thereof, in dealing with interpersonal relationships at home and at work.

Nothing will change — in either family — until this is done.

In the workplace, new systems can be introduced; new techniques can be tried. But the "batting averages" (average productive man-hours) will remain the same as they have been for the last half century until the troubled employee/wasted time problem is clearly understood and truly effective steps are taken to remedy the problem.

The right time to begin is immediately.
Delay is, as shown, extremely expensive.

(Figure 2)

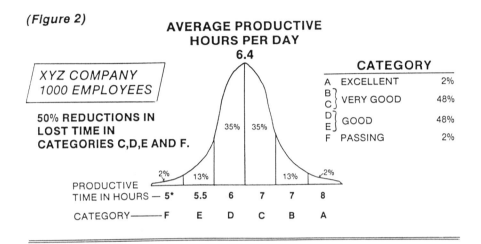

AVERAGE PRODUCTIVE HOURS PER DAY

CATEGORY		
A	EXCELLENT	2%
B C	VERY GOOD	48%
D E	GOOD	48%
F	PASSING	2%

XYZ COMPANY
1000 EMPLOYEES

50% REDUCTIONS IN LOST TIME IN CATEGORIES C,D,E AND F.

PRODUCTIVE
TIME IN HOURS — 5*   5.5   6   7   7   8

CATEGORY ——— F   E   D   C   B   A

(Table 2)
FORMULA FOR AVERAGE DAYS WORKED ANNUALLY:

DAYS OF THE YEAR	WEEKENDS	HOLIDAYS	VACATION	SICKDAYS	PERSONAL DAYS	DAYS WORKED ANNUALLY
365	104	8	12	8	3	230

CATEGORY	NO. OF EMPLOYEES	POSSIBLE HRS. PER DAY	HOURS LOST	POSSIBLE TOTAL DAILY PAYROLL	DAILY TOTAL DOLLAR LOSS TO COMPANY
A	20	160	—	$ 1,280	—
B	130	1040	130	8,320	$ 1,040
C	350	2800	350	22,400	2,800
D	350	2800	700	22,400	5,600
E	130	1040	325	8,320	2,600
F	20	160	60	1,280	480
	1000	8000	1565	$64,000	$12,520

PREVIOUS DAILY LOSS	$ 24,000
MODIFIED DAILY LOSS	$ 12,520
PREVIOUS ANNUAL LOSS	$5,520,000
MODIFIED ANNUAL LOSS	$2,879,600

TOTAL SAVINGS WITH A NEW MANAGEMENT-LABOR APPROACH - $2,640,400 ($5,520,000 - 2,879,600)

*Some will improve preformance.
Others will seek employment elsewhere.

27

The "HOME" Side

Of The Bridge

- Alcoholism
- Mate Selection
- Fear and Anger
- Destructive/Constructive Anger
- Who's in Charge?

ALCOHOLISM

Over 20 years ago, the American Medical Association defined alcoholism as a complex, progressive and fatal disease with specific symptoms. Still, many physicians continue to treat only the withdrawal syndrome, giving minimal or no attention to the emotional impairment of the alcoholic individual or the effects of alcoholism on the family unit.

Understanding alcoholism as a disease has been slow and difficult for many professionals and as a consequence, we have failed in too many cases to effectively help the victims. Alcoholism is not a moral weakness. It is an illness which is diagnosable and treatable. Left untreated, alcoholism is fatal. Statistically, untreated alcoholics die 12 years sooner than the general population.

During the course of unchecked alcoholism, the diseased persons and their significant others go through the same stages described by Dr. Elisabeth Kubler-Ross in her book, *Death and Dying:* denial and isolation; anger; bargaining, depression; and, hopefully, acceptance.

Pre-acceptance stages are unconscious defense mechanisms which protect the afflicted person against the fear of their condition. In the alcoholic, this protective mechanism, in addition to giving protection from fear, delays recognition and treatment, causing continued progression into advanced stages of the disease.

Alcoholism: The Disease Concept

The following exchange was reported in the Journal of the American Medical Association (JAMA) over 20 years ago:

Question: To the Editor: I have read much on the acceptance of alcoholism as a disease but have always felt that this is a moral or social problem rather than a medical one. I also feel that cirrhosis of the liver and psychosis would more likely have nutritional deficiency bases. Could you tell me what the grounds are for considering alcoholism as a medical illness? M.D., New York

Answer: A disease is defined as follows: In general, any deviation from a state of health; an illness or sickness; more specifically, a definite marked process having a characteristic train of symptoms. It may affect the whole body or any of its parts, and its etiology, pathology, and prognosis may be known or unknown.

It is important to note that the etiology and pathology may be known or unknown. It would be nice, but it is not necessary, to understand the etiology or pathology before dealing with the disease of alcoholism.

No attempt is being made here to aid in the diagnosis of alcoholism but before proceeding, we need to note at least some of the criteria used by the American Medical Association (AMA) in defining alcoholism. In the 1973 AMA Manual on Alcoholism, it is defined as follows:

Alcoholism is an illness characterized by preoccupation with alcohol and loss of control over its consumption such as to lead usually to intoxication if drinking is begun; by chronicity; by progression; and by tendency toward relapse. It is typically associated with physical disability and impaired emotional, occupational, and/or social adjustments as a direct consequence of persistent and excessive use of alcohol.

In short, alcoholism is regarded as a type of drug dependence of pathological extent and pattern, which ordinarily interferes seriously with the patient's total health and his adaptation to his environment.

Use of the Kubler-Ross model may be of help to professionals in identifying the proper areas for work with their patients as they understand better the stages of progression that alcoholics and their families go through in the active course of the disease.

Denial and Isolation Stage

Denial and isolation fortify alcoholics against their own fear about the increasing loss of control in their lives. However, it is difficult to camouflage fear and the spouse and other family members become frightened and restless themselves. This "fear vibration" ricochets back and forth among all the family members, intensifying it with each transference.

Alcoholics and their families go through no fewer than four steps of denial if the disease is left unchecked. If early detection of alcohol abuse occurs and is confronted, the disease can be arrested and there is no further progression of the series of denial steps and obviously the disease does not become terminal. Undetected, alcoholism will follow a four-step pattern of denial:

Step 1 of denial is culturally induced and reinforced. Patients actually do not perceive their drinking as in any way different from the majority of the general population.

Step 2 is experiential isolation. Alcoholics begin to experience symptomatic episodes which neither they nor their family members relate to each other. Each incident or situation is seen as a separate and distinct problem in itself, rather than a related pattern of experience which indicates an underlying cause.

Step 3 — Unconscious denial of alcoholism begins to produce conscious deceit. Patients deliberately lie about the quantity and frequency of alcohol consumption.

Step 4 — Denial has become so intense that patients develop an entire reality structure whose sole purpose is to protect and defend their alcoholism. At this point, denial is difficult to penetrate even for the trained therapist. The denial system is now pathological.

A brief development of the personal and social implications and ramifications of each step in the denial process will be helpful.

Step 1 — Lack of Perception

Most the U. S. drinking population is introduced to alcohol early in life. Pre-primers are often given sips of alcoholic beverages in a casual introduction to cultural mores. The visual media — television, movies, advertising photographs — show the use of alcohol as sophisticated, amusing and common. Our prevailing culture interferes with the perception of alcohol as potentially dangerous, addictive and fatal.

Early introduction to alcohol usually progresses no farther until adolescence when young teens begin experimenting with alcohol and quickly learn that it is an effective mechanism for dealing with emotions that are usually controlled by inhibition: timidity, aggression, inferiority, inadequacy, the sexual drive, anxiety, etc.

This use extends into adulthood and the drinking person is culturally comfortable. Drinking behavior blends in with the accepted cultural scene and the social camouflage is protective. In its denial of alcoholism as a disease, our culture places corrective emphasis only on the undesirable social effects of alcoholism and does very little toward treatment of the cause or catalyst of these effects. For instance:

- 80% of all wife abuse cases occur when the male has been drinking
- The majority of persons in jail are there on alcohol-related offenses
- 50% of all highway deaths are alcohol-related
- A significant number of rapists are under the influence of alcohol
- 50 to 75% of all divorces are alcohol-related.

The auto industry spends time and money on designing and producing safer cars while alcohol continues to produce unsafe drivers. The same kind of short-sightedness exists regarding marital abuse, rape, divorce and crime.

Even in marriage therapy, insufficient effort is made to identify abnormal drinking as a component or factor in marriage problems and treat it as an isolated variable; a problem in itself which may be either in addition to or related to other stated problems in the marriage.

Physicians and marriage and family therapists can be an important and valuable source of early diagnosis of alcoholism.

Both the alcoholic and the spouse lack the insight necessary for early detection because they fail to recognize any differences between their own behavior and that of the prevailing culture. The non-alcoholic spouse may feel that the alcoholic is insensitive, inconsiderate, inattentive and gives the family a low priority at times, but alcohol at this point is not perceived as a basic issue.

Step 2 – Experiential Isolation

Alcoholics, even when sober, have difficulty correlating one drinking episode with another. They do not see any relationship or progression in their drinking pattern. The alcoholic may have several episodes which, when viewed in isolation from each other, do not seem to deviate from the social norm. Therefore, to the patient, they have no cumulative significance. Consider the following case history:

Client A presents himself as an alert, well integrated and cooperative person who does not acknowledge a problem with alcohol. During the interview, the following is revealed: At age 15, the client was arrested for underage drinking. "But," he remarks, "I wasn't the only one." At age 17, and after abusing alcohol on other occasions, the client experienced his first blackout (lapse of memory) which, incidentally, he almost forgot to mention. At age 19, he was arrested on his first driving under the influence (DUI) charge.

He does not perceive the progressiveness and increasing seriousness of these episodes. When presented as a connected whole, the client at least began to consider the possibility of a problem with alcohol. Prior to the interview, his denial system kept each episode in isolation. With one having no connection with the others, it was much easier for him to rationalize each separate incident.

Additionally, the time parameters involved contribute to denial in the majority of cases. A destructive incident that occurs infrequently is easier to ignore or minimize than a series of sustained pattern of frequent behavior.

Spouses' need for everything to be all right will blind them to real issues and they also view each incident from an isolated and distorted perspective.

When barely noticeable differences finally expand and increase to a degree which cannot be ignored, this step in the denial process will no longer function adequately and the door opens to the next step.

Step 3 — Deceit

This step in the denial process involves conscious lying with a purpose. The alcoholic persons have become aware that their drinking is abnormal and that it is beginning to affect most areas of their lives. They are well entrenched in fear that they have a serious problem — which they still hope will go away — and the denial manifests itself in surreptitious drinking. The characteristically symptomatic *preoccupation* with alcohol has begun. Along with it is the beginning of impairment of functioning and further fragmentation of the family because the afflicted person begins to live in an internal world, shielded from external influences. Fear is engulfing the alcoholic and self-inflicted alienation begins.

Fear and love are not compatible; they cannot occupy the same space at the same time. Loss of the alcoholic's love generates fear in the spouse and children who then become preoccupied with their own fears. This compounds the disruption of the flow of family love and creates further alienation. If nothing is done to interrupt the process, the alcoholic's denial pattern advances to the most dangerous step.

Step 4 — Pathological

At this step in the denial process, alcoholics become delusional in reference to their drinking, lifestyle and relationships. They lose touch with reality. This delusional state is easy to camouflage since the culture itself manifests pathological delusions in its concerted efforts to remain oblivious to the ravages of this destructive disease. Drunkenness is amusing. Drunkenness is a personal right. Drunkenness is a "private" affair. As individuals minimize the effects of alcohol on their behavior, so does the society in which they live. As individuals attempt to prevent interference with their drinking, society cooperates with them.

Alcoholic people, even in this pathologically delusional denial state, are frightened by their own condition. They reveal enough residual healthiness to want to be rescued. Unfortunately, even professionnals seldom recognize the distress signals sent out by the patient.

37

Anger

For most people and for alcoholic families in particular, anger is a difficult emotion to deal with. It is also one of the least understood emotions.

Alcoholics' anger vacillates between anger that is appropriate, anger that is a disguise for fear, anger that is a disguise for guilt feelings, and anger disguised as hurt feelings. It is not surprising that we are unable to accurately identify these differences since, as children, adults continually encouraged us to alter our moods or feelings. If we were sad, we were told to cheer up; if we were too exuberant, we were told to calm down; if we were angry, we were told not to be; if we felt hurt, we were told not to take offense. It doesn't take very many years to begin camouflaging our real feelings and calling them something else or, worse, not even recognizing what we truly feel, as in the common remark, "I'm not sure how I feel."

Anger as Fear

Fear pervades every aspect of the alcoholic's life — fear of dependence, fear of failure, fear of intimate relationships, fear of parent role, fear of sexual performance — all of which develops into a generalized fear that these separate "threats" cannot be coped with and life will never be structured, stable and comfortable.

Alcoholics and their families, like anyone else, are afraid to be afraid and so fear is rarely acknowledged even to themselves, let alone verbally to other people. Anger is the most common disguise for fear. Alcoholics may be victims of any or all the fears mentioned. They are also afraid to call any of these fears by their right names. So they unconsciously disguise internal fears into behavior that is perceived externally by others as anger. It may take the form of irritability, inconsistency, exaggerated reactions to minor normal incidents, abusive language, and the like.

Fear is painful and alcoholics are like the wounded lion on a rampage, frightening all the animals around him until a little mouse removes the thorn in the lion's paw.

Alcoholics' family members react to the alcoholic's external behavior. They develop their own fears, confusions and acting out behavior. Spouses, sensing the onset of family fragmentation and loss of intimacy, may react with anger or withdrawal. Children may withdraw or begin acting out; e.g., school grades may drop or disciplinary problems become more frequent. The ricochet effect in the family is intensified. The alcoholic's fear and disguised-fear behavior has now generated fear in all the family members and they, too, are acting out fear disguised as something else — anger, punitive withdrawal, self-protective withdrawal, etc. And none of them recognize that their behavior is rooted in fear. They all think they are responding to anger with anger.

Anger Disguised As Hurt Feelings

Many people will not express anger overtly. Not only do people disguise fear as anger but they may also disguise anger in a passive way. For instance, instead of manifesting angriness, they may take refuge in "hurt feelings." We learn very early in life that in our society, anger is not an acceptable emotion. We are trained to feel guilty about sustained angriness. But there is no societal rule against hurt feelings. So our fears evoke anger and our anger is transformed into hurt feelings.

Anger Caused By Guilt

Angry behavior can also be a disguise for guilt feelings. When an undesirable drinking episode occurs, an attempt is made to suppress it and keep it hidden from others, much the same as a child who commits a forbidden act outside the home will then agitate his parents until he is finally reprimanded and the guilt is satisfied, even though the punishable act has been displaced. So with alcoholics who feel guilt about drinking. They will become restless and agitated and often provoke a quarrel with family members, thus relieving their guilt and justifying the act. This behavior confuses all family members; they withdraw; and fragmentation has increased.

Alcoholism has already caused enormous emotional damage to this family. The family members are fighting for their lives and the real enemy is still not visible.

Bargaining

In spite of not yet identifying alcoholism as the taproot of their problems, alcoholics and their families have already reached that stage in terminal illness which Kubler-Ross defines as bargaining. Alcoholics also go through a bargaining stage but unlike other terminally ill persons who feel that only God can heal them, alcoholics bargain with God, spouse, children, employer, therapist, and whomever will listen.

Attempts at modifying their behavior precede open bargaining. At first they may promise themselves not to drink too much at social gatherings. This is often successful but then periodically alcoholics will again drink more than they intended.

New bargaining techniques are tried — not drinking before a certain time of day or abstaining on work days and drinking only on weekends and even going a month or several months without drinking at all.

A bargaining dialogue goes on between family members. The alcoholic promises not to "overdo" it or not to drink at all; the spouse, often feeling partly or totally to blame, promises to do better; the children, feeling partly or totally to blame, either openly but more often privately attempt to modify their behavior so as not to "cause" the parent to drink.

The alcoholic goes through the motions of change without a real change in attitude. The body goes to AA or to church a few times or unacceptable behavior patterns are altered erratically. This external behavior without internal commitment is destined to fail and the alcoholic is more entrenched in the illness.

At this point, alcoholics and their families know perfectly well that something is seriously wrong. They have many problems and the family unit is in danger. Some will now recognize alcohol as a major or causative factor in their difficulties and many will not.

Just as other terminally ill persons want a miracle from God to heal them, alcoholics want an outside force to magically solve their problems. This bargaining with God is difficult for alcoholics since they already are afraid that God has forsaken them. Here we have the earliest detection of despair. They have reached the fourth stage in terminal illness: depression.

Depression

Kubler-Ross describes two kinds of depression: reactive and preparatory. Analogous to the depression experienced by the terminally ill in reaction to acute pain episodes, alcoholics experience reactive depression to acute drinking episodes. It is more apparent in someone with an obvious drinking problem who may go on a periodic binge which may last from 1 or 2 days to 1 or 2 weeks but it can also occur in someone who just overdoes it at a party or other social function.

This acute aftermath depression can be and often is present during earlier stages of the disease but is more likely to be camouflaged by reaction to physical symptoms such as hangover or by restlessness and/or agitation. In addition, when drinking episodes are brief, the alcoholic person recuperates quickly, recovers normal energy and stamina in a short time and thus more readily convinces themselves that there was, after all, nothing to get depressed about.

Mild depression of short duration becomes chronic depression and progresses first with a continual preoccupation with self and finally with an intensification of guilt, shame, fear, morbid ideas and now hopelessness.

The person who has heretofore been able to function adequately between drinking episodes now begins to deteriorate in all areas: productivity at work, creativity, interpersonal relationships and enjoyment of leisure time and activities. It is evident to the keen observer that detachment from the external environment has begun and is replaced with the person's internal world.

Morbid ideas are omnipotent. Suicide begins to take its toll. It has been reported that one of five alcoholic deaths is a result of suicide and 25% of all suicides are alcohol-related. As early as 1938, Karl Menninger, in his book *Man Against Himself*, listed alcohol addiction under chronic suicide. The National Institute on Alcohol Abuse and Alcoholism (NIAAA), in their book *Alcohol and Alcoholism*, used Menninger as a reference in calling alcoholism "suicide by inches." While alcoholism should not be thought of as a deliberate attempt at self-destruction, Dr. Menninger did focus early attention on premature death among those afflicted.

In addition, alcoholics' preoccupation and life in an internal world renders them vulnerable to the external environment in the form of personal neglect and susceptibility to a high frequency of accidents, some of which result in death. And death will occur prematurely if the person does not reach acceptance of the reality of alcoholism.

Acceptance

The entire family is now suffering from the ravages of the disease. The alcoholic, the spouse and the children have gone through their experiences of denial and isolation, anger, guilt, bargaining and depression. Proper understanding of the disease by the primary and secondary victims, with the help of professionals and various non-professionals, leads to acceptance which (unlike other terminal illnesses that culminate in death) leads to recovery.

It is impossible to identify exactly when, how or why alcoholics take the first step in acceptance. It appears that recovery is also a progressive process. There are characteristic stages in the development of alcoholism and there are characteristic stages in recovery from it.

Alcoholics and their families, going through the stages of progression into alcoholism, try various methods trying to find a way out of the labyrinth. Their bargaining system may have led them to try psychiatrists, pastors, AA, detoxing clinics, marriage therapists, medications, etc., in spite of which relapses occur. Eventually they will find that mode of treatment with which they are most comfortable and which produces the best results for them.

Unlike the laboratory maze which has only one correct exit, alcoholics may each find a different exit from alcoholism into a healthier life. But one common element seems to be that without the acceptance of total abstinence, relapse avoidance is impossible.

Not only must they relinquish the use of alcohol in any form but they must also relinquish all the various defense mechanisms so intensely cultivated during their progression into alcoholism. They must, in effect, give up the life they are now familiar with and begin a new kind of life.

This creates an extremely stressful situation. All people, alcoholic and nonalcoholic, experience acute stress when confronted with change and decision-making. It is frightening and it is resisted as long as the victim can endure or rationalize the pain – sometimes months, sometimes years, sometimes decades. But eventually the pain, as with physical pain in other terminal illnesses, will send the patient to seek treatment, no matter how frightening, threatening or stressful.

As in normal nonalcoholic decision-making, the decision itself has been preceded by a stage of preparation in which various alternatives are considered and tested before making the actual decision.

In this context, the bargaining stage in alcoholism can be seen not only as a stage of progression *into* alcoholism but also as an early preparatory stage in the decision to progress *out* of alcoholism.

Through a painful trial-and-error process, information is collected, experiments are tried, alternatives are tested, superficial adjustments are made, and eventually all possibilities are exhausted except one: admission of alcoholism and the decision to seek treatment.

The last vestige of bargaining takes place at this point. The person intellectualizes and objectifies alcoholism so as to keep it still "out there" and not "in here." Typically, alcoholics who initially seek and remain in treatment are almost excessively cooperative. They readily admit their alcoholism, they agree to whatever treatment the clinician suggests; they attend AA meetings; they keep their clinic appointments; they say all the "right" things.

There is external conformity but internal resistance to the necessity for designing and living a fundamentally new and different kind of life. Conforming is not the same thing as acceptance. And acceptance is what is needed for recovery to begin.

Conforming may develop into acceptance or it may crumble into relapse. In other words, conforming can be another type of bargaining which is still a stage *into* the disease, not a stage *out* of it.

Genuine acceptance and commitment to recovery has been reported by Dr. Harry Tiebout as an unconscious process. Even the patient cannot predict or explain clearly when, and why or how it happens. But that moment of relinquishing all defense mechanisms is necessary for treatment to be successful. When the patient is able to accept reality not only on the conscious level but also on the unconscious level, there is no further internal struggle and the patient experiences a radical relaxation with this freedom from stress and conflict.

The disease has been arrested and the victims have begun to heal.

Alcoholics' top priority is staying sober. They know that. Equally important, and equally difficult, alcoholics' family members must realize that sobriety takes precedence over all other goals. It is in everyone's best interest that the alcoholic stay sober.

Because of this emphasis on sobriety above all, Alcoholics Anonymous (AA) is sometimes falsely accused of being a recovery program based on selfishness. Everything in the alcoholic's life, including family members' needs, comes second to getting and staying sober.

Two things must be kept in mind:

- Putting sobriety first is not "selfish." Family members can't get any of the other things they want until the alcoholic stays sober. So sobriety comes first not only for the alcoholic's sake but also for the sake of the other family members. Nothing good happens for anyone until the alcoholic is, first, sober.

- Some alcoholics take advantage of "sobriety comes first" as an excuse to neglect their families. But the ones who do that soon wind up drinking again because selfishness and egocentricity are as self-destructive as booze.

When *un*selfish alcoholics put sobriety first, they consider both their own and their family's wellbeing. The very *lack* of selfishness helps the alcoholic maintain sobriety and make progress in recovery.

AA never has and never could advocate selfishness because selfishness works *against* recovery from alcoholism. Alcoholism is like a parasite in the person's body. The parasite feeds itself on selfishness and loneliness and then produces more selfishness and loneliness.

Selfishness is a lonely activity. Webster defines selfish as "concerned excessively or exclusively with oneself." What could be lonelier than that? Alcoholism is a lonely disease. To encourage selfishness is to promote loneliness.

All alcoholics will experience sustained loneliness in their active alcoholism and most have experienced loneliness for most of their lives. Selfishness in sobriety will jeopardize that sobriety because it isolates one from others and breeds the lonely feelings.

The only mission alcoholism has is to feed itself and it does so without regard to persons or things. As the disease progresses, the person manifests behavior characteristic of the disease and does so blindly. The alcoholic is labeled a "bad" person, an "immoral" person, a "weak" person. The alcoholic is unable to make others understand that the progressive weakening of their will and their and their sense of powerlessness is overwhelming and seemingly beyond their control.

Selfishness manifests itself in two ways: perceptibly, by absorbing money and time to support the disease and, in a less measurable way, by the emotional and mental detachment from family members.

Financial selfishness is usually not tested in the more affluent population but in the lower socio-economic group, the selfishness of the disease will often demand the purchase of alcohol before there is milk and cereal for the children.

Time selfishness is no respecter of socio-economic class. Time to drink and preoccupation with self is the same for the affluent as it is for the unemployed. If there is a need to drink, it will take priority over family, employment and all other activities.

Emotional and mental detachment also occurs at every socio-economic level. This detachment increases as the person submerges into the throes of the disease. The loss of confidence, the fear and the confusion grip the person and strangles them mentally and emotionally. They become increasingly concerned about self and eventually their entire existence is absorbed into alcoholism and its endless care and feeding. They are victims of an insidious and ravaging disease.

There are other victims. Spouse, children, parents and friends become victims. The family of an alcoholic suffers from the physical and emotional deprivation inflicted on them by the selfishness of alcoholism. They experience the anxiety of frequent financial crises. If they are not affluent, they experience the pain of embarrassment and sometimes the shame of poverty. If the alcoholic's pattern is to drink away from home, the family must suffer the pain of an absentee spouse or absentee parent. Even if the alcoholic drinks at home, the family has the impossible task of trying to interact with a person anesthetized by alcohol. When there is an alcoholic in the family, the pain and deprivation of emotional distance is always present.

Alcoholism eats away at an alcoholic's capacity for love, generosity, sensitivity, understanding another's feelings. Families need mutual emotional support; the sound, safe knowing that someone cares. They need affection, daily nurturing, positive verbal feedback, someone to depend on and trust. Most or all of these are denied them by the selfishness of rampant alcoholism.

Many non-alcoholic spouses and children are damaged so badly, so emotionally crippled by the effects of alcoholism in the family, that it often requires years to recover.

The day eventually arrives when the alcoholic makes a commitment to remain alcohol free. The alcoholic is apprehensive. The spouse is relieved. The children look on with confusion and wariness.

Alcoholics Anonymous becomes a necessary part of the recovery process. In some cases, 90 meetings in 90 days. In all cases, as many AA meetings as possible. Staying "dry" (alcohol free) is the name of the game. Don't take a drink today. Nothing must interfere with sobriety for without it, the alcoholic has no hope. The program *must* take priority.

Unfortunately, the phrase "selfish program" is frequently substituted for program of priority. Selfish is what fed the disease. Selfish is what alienated family members. Selfish destroys self-image and confidence. Selfish will do all that in recovery too if the alcoholic's attitude is merely "I must take care of me because I'm first; I'm number one." Selfishness, even in recovery, is loneliness. Loneliness is dangerous to an alcoholic and the family.

As relieved as the spouse is that abstinence is working, the spouse contintinues to feel rejected and alone. As relieved as the children are that the parent is not drinking, there is still parental absenteeism and neglect. The family continues to be afraid, cautious and angry.

They are afraid and angry because there has been little understanding and support for them. Al-Anon cannot do it. A therapist cannot do it. Al-Anon and therapist can only help the spouse and family to understand why the alcoholic can't or won't do it.

Genuine relief to the family comes when the alcoholic acknowledges that the recovery program must take priority. It must be done with the attitude that all members of the family are important and all members have been scarred by the disease of alcoholism. All must understand that a lot of time will be required to recover and many meetings will have to be attended.

Alcoholics and their families must understand and agree on two things basic to their common wellbeing:

- Sobriety is sacred if the diseased life is to heal.
- Without sobriety, the family will remain emotionally fragmented, battered, nonfunctional.

Do not allow the program of recovery to become a selfish program because selfishness breeds loneliness and loneliness is an enemy to the alcoholic.

Do make the program a program of priority for sobriety is the only chance there is to begin restoring all the shattered lives to wholeness.

Supervisor / Parent
of Business and Industry

$\mathcal{VQC}$ says: Alcoholism is an insidious disease. Most families miss the early symptoms. If someone in your family drinks too much or causes problems when they do drink, seek help for yourself and learn what to do about it.

Early Morning Scene

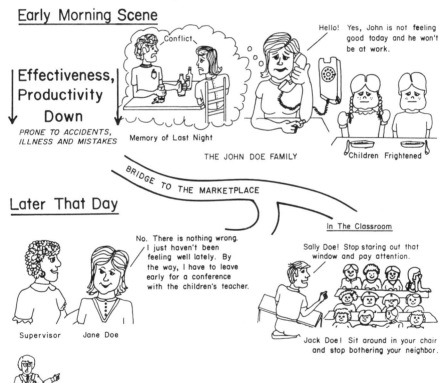

Effectiveness, Productivity Down

PRONE TO ACCIDENTS, ILLNESS AND MISTAKES

Conflict

Memory of Last Night

THE JOHN DOE FAMILY

Hello! Yes, John is not feeling good today and he won't be at work.

Children Frightened

BRIDGE TO THE MARKETPLACE

Later That Day

No. There is nothing wrong. I just haven't been feeling well lately. By the way, I have to leave early for a conference with the children's teacher.

Supervisor   Jane Doe

In The Classroom

Sally Doe! Stop staring out that window and pay attention.

Jack Doe! Sit around in your chair and stop bothering your neighbor.

$\mathcal{VQC}$ says: People have a tendency to hide serious problems. Please don't do that to yourself. Reach out for help. The sooner you detect and confront a problem the easier it is to resolve.

49

MATE SELECTION

Love has many definitions, some of which are vague, sentimental, distorted, unrealistic or childish. The biblical definition is a good one. A professional psychologist might say that love is kind; love is sensitive; love is caring, gentle, generous, patient, affectionate, playful, compassionate. It is a willingness to be open and sharing at a feeling level. Above all, love is trusting. It is not possible to have even a good relationship, let alone a loving relationship, without mutual trust. These love components will be found wherever there is love between two people. The two people may be parent and child. Friends. Lovers. Husband and wife.

The love between husband and wife is probably the most difficult to preserve, develop and sustain. If the emotional, sexual and intellectual intimacy of marriage is to last a lifetime, it must be continually cultivated as one would tend a fragile plant to keep it growing and flourishing.

Most people enter marriage excited and full of hope for a lasting, happy marriage. Many find, a few years later, that honeymoon feelings and expectations have faded. The marriage has wilted. Dried up. It no longer produces new growth.

Other people enter marriage more as missionaries than as spouses. "I thought he would change after we got married." People don't change just because they get married. Behavior patterns are set early in life and continue through adulthood unless something dramatic interrupts that pattern and causes a change in course.

Our behavior patterns, our choices at "choosing points" in our lives, depend largely on whether or not our needs are being met. These needs are common to all people, defined by Abraham Maslow as:

1) Food
2) Shelter and security
3) Love
4) Self-esteem

Biological needs are not too difficult to satisfy in this country where few people starve to death. Safety needs would not be a major concern either if the need for love and self-esteem were not so often unfulfilled. There is a statistical correlation between love deprivation/low self-esteem and the number of highway, home and industrial accidents and poor physical fitness which can lead to heart problems and other diseases.

Love and self-esteem are not "extras" in human life; they are basic needs. If they are so important and desirable, why are they so often elusive? Why, for instance, do people fall in love with partners who later reject them? How do people find each other?

The Selection System

Each of us has a unique internal selection system that determines the kind of person we will be attracted to. When we meet people, we register instantaneous reactions to them. Our internal selection system is automatic. This person is attractive. That one isn't. We are indifferent to some others. Before we think and analyze, before we accumulate additional information, our selection system has already sorted people into those who meet our unconscious, unfulfilled needs and those who don't. These needs are what "turn us on."

At a party, a man will notice some women and not others. The man believes that he is attracted to women who are pretty, shapely, bright, amusing, kind, artistic or athletic. If you asked him, that is what he would say.

Suppose that this man is a dependent kind of person. His need to be dependent subconsciously "screens" the women in the room for one who will allow herself to be depended upon. That is what really attracts him.

Suppose the "selected" woman at this party has a strong need to take care of other people and perhaps men in particular. Her selection system quickly locates the dependent man. The attraction is obviously mutual.

No matter how independent each behaves at first, it is only a matter of time before they assume their needed roles — he in his dependency and she in her caretaking and controlling.

This couple may feel very happy and in love at first. But being helpless and being controlling puts them both in a no-win situation. He is dependent but at the same time resents his dependence. She figuratively likes to "carry" him but at the same time she gets tired and resents the burden.

They begin to develop a love/hate relationship. Loving the unhealthy need being fulfilled (his helplessness, her mothering) but hating each other for allowing it to happen.

Helplessness/mothering is not a healthy relationship for adults. The day comes when they wonder why they ever got married. That awakening is not sudden but slow and painful. It is preceded by open or silent criticism, often about trivial matters.

One doesn't like the way the other parks the car, arranges the furniture, drops clothes on the floor, chews with their mouth open, or (proverbially) leaves the cap off the toothpaste.

This is all "sounding brass and tinkling cymbals." The criticism and repeated potshots are really a manifestation of their unhappiness and buried resentment, their sense of deprivation, their low opinion of themselves, their fear that they may never find the key to a happy, contented life. They are restless, frustrated and frightened and, therefore, angry. They become preoccupied with their own inner strife. This unresolved conflict affects the whole family. It crosses the bridge to the marketplace where, as employees, they are prone to mistakes, accidents and inefficiency. Not because they are bad people or bad employees but because they feel so deprived and negative about themselves.

Their selection system was flawed to begin with.

Carrie was a dark-haired child in a Scandinavian family noted for blond hair and blue eyes. She was the older of two girls. The younger sister did have blond hair and blue eyes. She also developed an easy, outgoing charm and excelled in both her studies and athletics. Compared with her younger sister, Carrie never quite measured up and she began to distance herself from the family. With her dark hair, she was literally the "black sheep" of the family.

Carrie has an understandably low self-esteem. In her instinctive drive to improve that self-esteem, she "decided" that there was something she could be very good at that no one could take away from her. She could be a good mother. It didn't take her long to get started. At age 16, she became pregnant and married. Getting pregnant served two purposes. It got her out of the family house which she considered hostile to her and launched her on her quest to be happy and proud of herself as a superstar mother.

Several years and four children later, Carrie found herself in an unhappy marriage to an alcoholic husband and with many doubts about her parenting skills. She didn't believe that her children loved her. She felt that she had failed at the one thing she had been so sure she could do superlatively well — be a good mother.

What went wrong? How had her selection system interfered with reaching her chosen goal?

Carrie was unsure of herself because of the verbal and emotional abuse that she had experienced at home. To ensure that she would stand out as a good parent, she unconsciously selected a man who was so emotionally deprived that he became totally preoccupied with himself. The early signs of alcohol abuse were ignored and soon into the marriage, Carrie's husband was deep in the throes of alcoholism. The responsibility for raising the children fell on Carrie's shoulders – just the way she "needed" it to be.

The unconscious maneuver is uncanny. The worse parent the husband became, the more it fell on Carrie to be super-Mom. Her "plan" was being fulfilled.

Still, she did not feel comfortable, secure, confidant and proud of herself, as she had planned and expected from motherhood.

In order to reinforce her role as the "good" parent, she subconsciously provoked arguments between the children and their father. When he then became verbally or physically abusive with them, she would intercede to protect them.

Her tactics were self-defeating. She felt guilt about the provocation and when the children were hurt, it was as though she had done the abusing. To an observer, she appeared to be the rescuing heroine. To herself, in the privacy of her feelings, she was a bad, unacceptable person. She did indeed exploit and manipulate her husband and children for her own distorted purposes, not because she was bad but because her desperate effort to feel important and acceptable had dominated her life and behavior since childhood. She was not really trying to be a mature adult/good mother. She was still trying to become an acceptable child. And didn't know it.

All relationships are not as complex and damaging as Carrie's. Chad and Betty met as youngsters and married in late adolescence. Betty was the daughter of an alcoholic father. She lived with her mother and two brothers. She saw herself as special in her father's eyes even though he was out of the house most of her life and drinking most of the time when he was home.

Chad's father died when Chad was four. His mother put him in a foster home. He grew up with the image that people "eventually leave you." After all, his father left him (through death) and his mother abandoned him.

To protect himself from emotional pain and love loss, Chad

became a rigid and emotionally guarded person. He shared little with Betty. He spent a lot of time alone or out of the house. Sexual activity was infrequent. He was a good man and a good provider, yet Betty felt emotionally deprived. The more she tried to establish intimacy and sharing between them, the more he withdrew — as her father had done when she was a child.

Chad didn't drink but he did keep her at a distance. If Betty complained or nagged or made demands, he would concede, "Why don't you find someone else?"

His lifelong expectation that people would leave him was affecting his adult relationship. It was as if he had to fulfill the prophecy by getting Betty so discouraged that she would leave him.

They seemingly selected each other to play out the same roles they had played as young children.

Their internal selection systems had acted through their unmet needs to attract them to each other. Both of them wanted their marriage to succeed. They decided to seek the help of a marriage counselor. It took them two years of therapy to fully understand the how and why of what was happening to them, to come to comfortable terms with their pasts, and to learn new, healthy, adult ways to deal lovingly with each other and with their children.

Our selection systems are often misleading and flawed by events over which we had no control. But if we make the effort necessary to learn and understand the internal dynamics at work, the stories of our life-choices can have happy endings.

We can rescue not only our own lives but the lives of our children. After we work out the kinks in our selection systems, we make better choices and better decisions, whether as spouses, parents, employers or employees. We lead happier, more productive lives, both at home and at work.

FEAR AND ANGER

Fear and anger are closely related. They even have the same physical symptoms. Rapid pulse, sweating, trembling, change in voice pitch, elevated blood pressure and acute anxiety. A very uncomfortable set of feelings in either case.

When we are frightened, we have only two basic choices — retreat from the threat or face it. This is the classic primitive choice of "fight or flight."

In the animal kingdom, creatures who are threatened and afraid literally run for their lives or fight for their lives.

Human beings have subtler, more complex ways of dealing with fear. We can withdraw emotionally (flight) or display anger (fight). Neither silence nor scenes deal with the real problem — fear.

Getting angry is a perfectly natural, even instinctive, reaction to being threatened and feeling afriad. If we are the object of someone's anger, we feel threatened by them and we react by becoming angry with the person who is "attacking" us. That then makes *two* angry people.

Meeting anger with anger is not going to get anyone anywhere because it doesn't deal with the underlying problem — fear of something.

Granted, it is very difficult to remain calm and coolheaded and logical when someone is shouting at us. If, in the split second before we shout back, we can ask ourselves "What is this person afraid of?", we can manage to avoid most screaming matches. There are no winners in screaming matches. They produce only wounds and damage.

Anger is not the problem. Fear is the problem.

Bosses who snap at assistants about incomplete data are really worried about the emergency staff meeting. They are afraid they'll look inadequate if they don't have all the facts. Because they're afraid, they show anger.

If the assistants can manage not to respond instantly with anger over being snapped at, if they can recognize the boss' fear for what it is, then together they are quite likely to collect everything they need for the meeting in plenty of time.

Likewise, if assistants and staff people are angry with the boss about something, the boss should think "What are they afraid of?". The answer to that question contains the real information needed to resolve the situation satisfactorily.

The same principle applies to spats and friction between husbands and wives, parents and children, labor and management, neighbor and neighbor.

Parents who get angry with a child about poor grades or bad manners are reacting to several fears. They are afraid the child will wind up ill-educated, impolite, inadequate to meet social and academic demands and standards in later life. It's the child's future they're fearful of.

Parents are also afraid that their children will be an embarrassment to them in front of relatives, neighbors or friends. The child's behavior threatens the parents with "loss of face." No one likes to be embarrassed, humiliated or made to look foolish.

On the whole, children cannot be expected to recognize the fears behind their parents' anger. Children can't even imagine angry parents as frightened people.

With other adults, it may not be unreasonable to hope for some understanding that anger is a symptom—twin of fear but that is far too much to ask of a child. So it is particularly important for angry parents to ask themselves "What are we afraid of?".

Losing one's temper and shouting or snapping or cursing at other people is a maneuver for control. Withdrawing affection is also a maneuver for control. In these situations, asking "What are you sore about?" is the wrong question. The right question is "What are you afraid of?".

DESTRUCTIVE/CONSTRUCTIVE ANGER

Anger and love are incompatible emotions. They cannot occupy the same space at the same time. Anger is the dominant emotion and can eventually obliterate love altogether.

Everyone gets angry, some more quickly and intensely than others, but no one is immune from anger. How effectively anger is dealt with determines how much or how little love one is able to give and to receive.

In any relationship, the level of lovingness is directly correlated to the level of unresolved anger. The major cause of "distance" in relationships is unresolved anger.

People usually handle their anger in one of four ways:

- Some seem to be irritated all the time and they get angry over the most trivial matters. If their anger is more passively expressed, they will be constantly hypercritical of everyone and everything.
- Some people seem never to get angry and say that they never do.
- Others are "slow to anger" meaning that they restrain anger until it becomes unmanageable and then they explode.
- Only a few are able to express their anger clearly without physically or verbally abusing other people or retracting affection and respect previously given.

The first three responses block the "channels of love." Only the last does not.

The person who seems constantly angry usually knows it but doesn't really know what to do about it. Commonly, this type of person has been a victim of childhood neglect and emotional or physical abuse. They may shrug it off as normal and say, "That's the way I am." Others may accept that "that's the way he is." They make adjustments and accept the emotional distance that such behavior causes.

As a temporary measure, accepting and "going around" such behavior may be reasonable and workable, particularly if one seldom comes in contact with such a person. But if the person is your spouse, this method of "getting along" is too one-sided to last long. It contains the classic beginnings of serious marital problems.

Approaching a perpetually angry person is frightening. Fear and love don't mix. Romantic feelings fade fast when one person must always tiptoe carefully around another in order to avoid angry tirades.

Under such circumstances, the best one can hope for is a life of defensive maneuvers. And they won't work very long because the person on the defensive is getting more and more angry about having to be so defensive.

Beyond the damage to romance, couples with children must consider the effect of a continuously smoldering parent on a child. Children are often blamed, both directly and subtly, for being the cause of the anger they feel around them. Their reactions to being "under attack" are usually extreme. They either get poor grades in school or become a driven overachiever; they openly rebel or become "goody two shoes." And always there is the hopeless feeling that they don't know how to penetrate the wall between them and the angry parent. They initially feel that nothing they do is acceptable. Then they feel that they are not an acceptable person. The love channel between parent and children is solidly blocked.

In contrast is the "never get angry" person. What this really means is "never let the anger show." Everyone gets angry and anger always blocks love to some degree. With this type of person, the anger is camouflaged. The person seems to be totally cooperative, always blameless, never upset. This angry person may develop a strong sex drive to cover up the emotional distance created by hidden anger. How can you say that they aren't "loving" when they always want you sexually? The never-angry person never finds fault with the children. Everything is always okay with them. Such undiluted acceptance sounds good until one realizes that acceptance loses its meaning when everything is acceptable. It's like saying that everyone is special. By definition, if everyone is special, no one is special.

The "never get angry" person expresses anger passively in a variety of ways — by agreeing to something and then not doing it, by procrastination on projects, by tardiness. This behavior upsets you frequently enough to trigger your own anger but makes it difficult to express toward such a "nice" person. A person who never openly expresses anger may give love intellectually but not intimately. Love can't flow back and forth between people when one or both of them is building up a dam of hidden anger. The relationship will eventually rupture.

Then there are the slow to anger people. They tend to declare this with a note of pride. What they really mean is that they hold back anger until it overwhelms them and then they erupt. Woe to all within range.

These eruptions are usually triggered by the sense of loss of control. The outburst of anger is to get everyone back into line and thus regain the feeling of control.

Approaching a person like this is akin to crossing a minefield. You had better proceed carefully and endure the anxiety if you want to make it through the encounter without mishap. People who live with a slow-to-anger person aren't in constant turmoil as are those who live with the perpetually angry. But they do have to continually scan the environment for clues to the next eruption.

In this case, love is blocked by the sporadic eruptions and is impeded both prior to and for some time after the blow-up. If these outbursts occur too frequently, they can permanently block the love flow. The poor partner never gets enough time to recover a sense of lovingness.

To enjoy the fullness of love, it is necessary to run the risk of telling others what irritates you and what offends you; to acknowledge and share your "sore spots" and be willing to work together on changing the habits and attitudes that are disrupting your life and blocking the channels needed for the easy-flowing exchange of love.

The continually angry person, with the cooperation of a caring and understanding partner, can change. Perhaps a skilled therapist may be needed to unearth the real source of the anger and help the person talk about it, understand it and finally abandon it.

The "never gets angry" person can stop denying anger and discover that it is possible to express anger and still be a nice person.

The "slow to anger" person needs to learn that minor irritations must be aired and resolved before they build up into a major outburst of rage.

"Expressing anger" is not a license for ridicule, insults, blame-placing or sarcasm. It is not a name-calling contest or a shouting match. Above all, it is not an excuse to hurt the other person's feelings. Expressing anger is a cooperative effort to resolve an *issue* that causes anger.

There are two commandments for expressing anger:
- Explain the problem and its effect on your feelings.
- Remember that you're not opponents, you're two people trying to solve a problem that affects both of you.

If any two people can cooperate in such an effort, they can dissolve the anger-block and clear the channels for renewed love, respect, trust and sharing.

VQC says: "Unresolved anger blocks love in the home and reduces effectiveness and productivity in the marketplace."

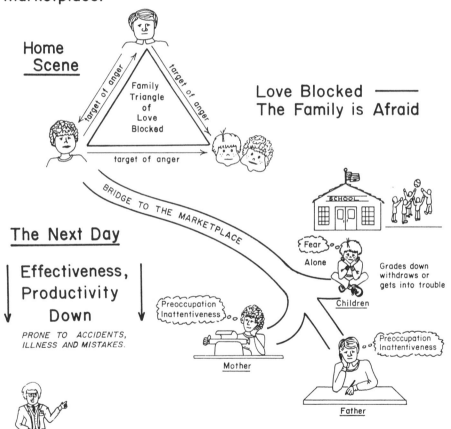

Home Scene

target of anger

target of anger

Family Triangle of Love Blocked

target of anger

Love Blocked ——— The Family is Afraid

BRIDGE TO THE MARKETPLACE

The Next Day

Effectiveness, Productivity Down

PRONE TO ACCIDENTS, ILLNESS AND MISTAKES.

Preoccupation Inattentiveness

Mother

Fear Alone

Grades down withdraws or gets into trouble

Children

Preoccupation Inattentiveness

Father

VQC says: "No one likes to be deprived of love. No one likes to be unhappy. If your family can't resolve the issues that separate you, seek assistance."

65

WHO'S IN CHARGE?

No one can control another person's behavior for very long. It's like compressing a spring. The tighter the spring is compressed, the stronger the rebound will be. People react the same way to efforts to pressure them into changing their behavior.

A couple on the beach were behaving rather oddly. . .

They looked no different than all the other young couples around them. The man was stretched out on his stomach, dozing. The woman was reading. The children were building sand castles.

The man sat up, the woman poured him a glass of orange drink, he gulped the drink and resumed his nap. The woman glanced at him and then hastily poured some orange drink from the container into the sand. Each time the man asked for more orange drink, the woman gave it to him and then, when he wasn't looking, poured some into the sand.

The orange drink contained vodka, the man was getting drunk, and the wife was trying to control his behavior by spilling some of his supply.

The same sort of attempted control goes on in millions of homes every day. Some wives pour half a bottle of liquor down the drain and refill the bottle with water. Some husbands mix drinks for their wives with a minimum of liquor and a maximum of water or mixer. Some spouses "accidentally" drop and break or throw away bottles of liquor.

Some make threats, cut off money, enlist children as confidants and allies, or use silence, anger and guilt as weapons to control the other's behavior. None of these "pressure" tactics will work for very long.

It is frightening to have an alcohol abuser in the family. It is utterly futile to try to control that person's drinking.

Abusive or uncontrolled drinking is the drinker's problem. The need to control someone else's behavior is the "controller's" problem. We cannot control or change anyone's behavior except our own.

It is just as frightening to have employees who are uncooperative and may even believe that rules and standards do not apply to them. Many supervisors try to control a staff member's behavior by making implicit or explicit threats. This is futile unless the supervisor is willing to follow through with that threat. In fact, the more often threats are made without follow through, the more confident the offenders are that they can do what they want without consequences.

The need or urge to control another's behavior is a sure sign that we have lost control of the course and quality of our own life and allowed someone else to dictate whether we shall be happy or unhappy.

The way out of this senseless situation is to stop reacting to the other person's behavior entirely. Give up all attempts to control their behavior. Their behavior is *their* problem, *their* responsibility.

"REPAIRS AND MAINTENANCE"- A Comprehensive Program

- Introduction
- Education–Staff and Families
- Training Workshops– Staff and Families
- Peer Support Group Training–Supervisory Personnel

INTRODUCTION

American business and industry is suffering serious economic blight. A major cause of this blight has its roots in gradual but progressive decomposition of the domestic family unit. Families are becoming more alienated, frightened and angry. The working members of these families cross an imaginary bridge to enter the doors of business and the gates of industry every shift of every day. These alienated, frightened and angry family members assume their roles in the business/industrial complex in every echelon of every company.

Finding and solving the problems has eluded management. First, most people deal with their anxiety and express their anger passively in covert activity, making it extremely difficult to recognize and influence. Secondly, everyone from company president to janitor contributes to the problem by shifting blame, which only enables the blight to progress.

Management with good intentions, has persistently lacked insight and sensitivity to the hidden messages of misbehavior. To compensate for this lack, they have directed their energy toward measurable performance. This practice measures effects without even attempting to recognize causes.

Training programs are a familiar part of the American business scene. Future industrial leaders are groomed for their progression up the corporate ladder. The more affluent the enterprise, the

71

more elaborate the training; but the programs share a common flaw. They concentrate on specific job training and fail to examine the trainees' ability to cope with personal and domestic problems.

People can be trained to perform a vast array of tasks commensurate with their abilities. But so can pigeons. Clearly, management woes lie beyond technical training. The training necessary to reverse the trend is directly related to how effectively employees manage personal and domestic problems because that is where business problems come from. Faulty, inadequate coping skills preclude top performance in the marketplace. Unfortunately, most management people have been inadequately prepared for peak job performance.

A group of psychology students chose a "rat race" as a fund raising project. Each student had two weeks to train their rat to navigate a maze as quickly as possible. Each student expected their rat to win.

On the afternoon of the race, exuberant spectators paid their admission and crowded into the room, cheering, shouting and whistling. The bell sounded, the doors of the starting gates opened, and a startling thing happened. All but one of the rats froze in their starting position. Only one easily completed the course and won the race.

The winner was no "super-rat." He succeeded because his training environment had simulated that of the actual race. The trainer had invited friends to each practice run so the rat was conditioned to the noise of the spectators. The other rats had been trained in the quiet of isolated rooms.

Management must realize that most people are no more fortunate than the immobilized rats; success eludes all who are ill prepared for it.

People can be trained to lower their stress levels. They can be trained in supervisory techniques. Their technical training can be *par excellence* but until management understands the behavioral patterns which cause stress and other negative responses, they will be plagued by personnel problems. They will continue to experience rampant absenteeism, accidents and sabotage. The immeasurable level of employee preoccupation will continue to cost billions of dollars each year in the form of slowed production, project delays, and mistakes. Basic human needs must be understood and met before success can be realized.

A comprehensive program that reaches both sides of the "bridge" simultaneously will have to be adopted. It must transcend all other human resource programs that exist today.

This comprehensive program must be two-pronged. Education and training. The education part of the program must include both pictorial and written messages that focus directly on real interpersonal situations to enable employees and families to identify with and to correlate the behavior of the domestic family with the business/industrial family.

Lectures are also an important part of the educational program. Topics are not limited but they must include at least these six subjects:

1) Parenting
2) Couples Growing Together
3) Communication
4) Human Sexuality
5) Coping with Anger
6) Alcoholism

The second prong is training. Training given in the form of workshops gives an experiential perspective of domestic situations. It prepares employees and their family members to cope more effectively with their anger as well as the anger of others. It helps them to understand and deal with their own fear as well as the fears of others. It helps to encourage them when once they were discouraged. Training will help them to see and experience the benefits of their achievement. It will create new awareness of the consequences, both negative and positive, of their behavior. It will offer new options in difficult situations. All of these changes will give a new security and a new confidence to those who choose to use the training.

Various training workshops may be offered but the most important and essential are these four:

1) Parenting
2) Couples Growing Together
3) Human Sexuality
4) Alcoholism.

Communications and coping with anger, which are two of the lectures, are not dealt with as separate training experiences because they are included in both the Parenting workshop and the Couples Growing Together workshop.

Finally, a Peer Support Group (PSG) for supervisors should be initiated. The group is designed to help each other cope with the complexities of personnel problems. Such a group will develop new confidence and skills in all the supervisory participants.

TRUST

One of Robert Frost's poems reads:

I have miles to go
And promises to keep
Before I sleep.

Keeping promises is the most basic of all "social contracts" between people. Individuals must be able to trust other individuals; groups must be able to trust other groups; or the fundamental gears of society grind to a halt.

It is impossible to have a good life, a good relationship, a good business, or a good society without an unshakeable foundation of mutual trust. We must keep the promises we make. Our word must be trustworthy or ultimately society itself crumbles.

Mutual trust is built gradually, based on past experience, and remains always fragile. It doesn't take much to demolish trust between people or groups. One lie, one broken promise, one excuse to renege on an agreement is enough to shatter trust that may be years old.

Learning about trust begins early. Sometimes parents promise a child something just to put an end to whining and pestering. When the time comes to keep the promise, they make excuses, even perfectly valid excuses. But the child has learned that parents don't always do what they say they're going to do. Their word alone is not really reliable. Maybe they will keep promises; maybe they won't. Maybe they will actually carry out a threatened punishment and maybe they won't. Children will keep testing until they find out exactly what they can depend on as true and reliable.

Adults do the same thing. We never outgrow our need to continually determine what and who is trustworthy.

Trustworthiness often rests on "minor" matters like being on time. Making an appointment is a promise to another person. Someone trusts us to keep our word. If we're late, we break a promise and abuse that trust. The other person will not forget. Trust once betrayed is never easy to restore.

Mutual trust is the most essential element in all relationships — husband/wife, child/parent, teacher/student, management/labor, citizen/government. Each must be able to believe what the other says or no functioning relationship is possible. We avoid people who renege on their word. We are wary of people who lie to us even once.

To create and sustain trustworthiness, we have to *mean* what we say and *do* what we say we're going to do.

We all have "promises to keep."

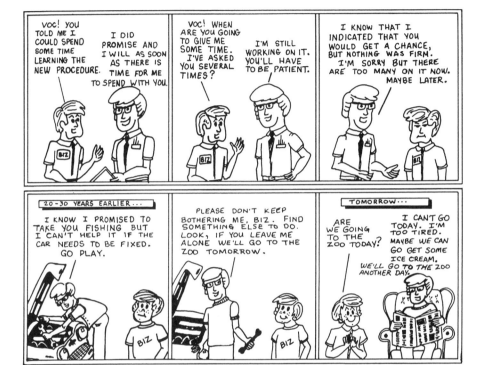

DANGER! CONFIDENTIAL!

Conversations that begin, "Confidentially. . . ." are rarely about good news. Confidants should be wary. Something is afoot and the confidant is getting caught up in someone else's "battle." The speaker is, more likely than not, lining up "allies" and the confidant will be pressured into choosing "sides" in the other person's problem. Let the confidant beware.

The one, unbreakable rule for sound, effective relationships is, "Talk *to* people; not *about* people."

If parents have some grievance to settle between them, they should talk *to* each other; not *about* each other to the children, to relatives or to the neighbors. Arguments, disagreements, gripes and dissatisfactions between parents cannot be resolved by lining up the "votes" of outsiders, including children. Especially children.

Using a friend as a confidant solely to malign some third person is shameful abuse and exploitation of that friend. The confidant is being pressured to agree in the defamation of another person's character. To disagree puts the "friendship" at risk. Any sensible person will resent the attempt.

Using children as confidants in a battle between parents qualifies as cruelty to children.

One parent may feel "defeated" in an argument with the other and then turn to the children as allies in hope of "victory" over the spouse. Poor children. They love both parents and when they are caught in the middle between parents and asked to condemn one, they become frightened and angry.

If the children agree with one parent, they may offend the other. If they disagree, they fear loss of love or parental retaliation. In most cases, the children withdraw from both parents until the storm blows over. If children are placed in this cruel situation too often, their withdrawal from their parents may become permanent and irreversible.

The same principles apply to the business/industrial family. The roles and purposes may be different but the dynamics are the same. Divide and conquer. Stir up friction and suspicion. Line up allies.

Workers use other workers. Coworkers try to enlist supervisors. Supervisors use staff members and other supervisors. All are involved in using people to gain or consolidate power and get the upper hand in some problematic situation.

The price is high. Forcing people into divided loyalties creates fear and anger. Fear creates tension, uncertainty, suspicion and worry, followed inevitably by an increase in accidents and mistakes on the job.

Anger can even arouse revenge which would be manifested in industrial sabotage: slowed production, direct and purposeful damage to product and equipment, petty theft, an increase in lost time through illness and apathy.

The solution is the same for both the domestic family and the business/industrial family.

Be honest, clear and direct about grievances or dissatisfaction. Any conflict can be resolved to full, mutual agreement by reasonable people. A sense of humor will help enormously in the process.

An agreement does not produce winners and losers. It produces only winners. Agreement means that all parties concerned feel satisfied with the solution they have mutually arrived at.

V℺C Supervisor / Parent of Business and Industry

BY: Bob Nass

PARENTS CONFLICT

LATER... I NEVER GET CREDIT AROUND HERE. YOU BOTH KNOW HOW IT IS, ETC.

EVEN LATER..

I NEVER GET COOPERATION. YOU KNOW WHAT I'M TALKING ABOUT.

VOC—BIZ CONFLICT

LATER... (TO OTHER WORKERS) YOU KNOW HOW DIFFICULT BIZ CAN BE, ETC.

EVEN LATER..

(TO COWORKERS) VOC ALWAYS HAS TO HAVE THINGS HIS WAY, ETC.

—CRITIQUE—

TO PARENTS! Never use children as con-fidants. It will fright-en them and they resent being put in the middle of those they love.

TO VOC AND BIZ! Never use coworkers as confidants. It has a demoralizing effect on all concerned.

TO ALL! Identify the issue and negotiate it to mutual satisfaction. If you cannot do it together, seek the assistance of an appropriate third party.

DOWN IN THE DUMPS

When Employee A "dumps" his work on Employee B and gets away with it, Employee B holds Supervision responsible for tolerating the behavior of Employee A. And rightly so.

This situation is similar to a home in which one youngster repeatedly skips out on his chores, leaving them for a brother or sister, and the parents do nothing about it. The dumped-on child blames the parents more than the brother.

At work, "dumping" creates several problems for supervisors. One is their own anxiety about having to confront Employee A and also get him to willingly and reliably do his fair share of work in the future. Anxiety about a confrontation makes a person tend to put off dealing with the problem.

If the supervisors just ignore the situation, they tacitly encourage Employee A to keep on dumping. Employee B begins to look for ways to "get even" with the supervisor/company for not correcting the situation. The morale of other employees goes down as they too feel threatened by the supervisor's failure to cope with the problem. And the supervisors, aware of their own procrastination, suffer lowered self-confidence and self-esteem. Unsolved problems thus breed more and bigger problems.

Supervisors at any level need to make it clear to "dumpers" that employment is a contract between employer and employee to get certain specified work done. The employer agrees to deliver the pay; the employee agrees to deliver the work.

Responsible adults abide by the terms of their contracts.

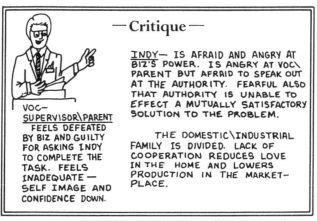

BLAME GAMES

One of the major causes of friction and discord between people, at home or at work, is the largely subconscious struggle for power — between married couples, between parents and children, between management and labor.

Those involved don't usually recognize the problem as a power struggle. They perceive most conflict or disruption only in terms of someone's "fault" so the struggle for power (Who's right? /Who's wrong?/Who wins?/Who loses?) is camouflaged as "blame."

The classic situation is labor trying to get as much as possible while doing as little as necessary and management trying to get as much as possible while giving as little as necessary. Then each blames the other for the resultant discord.

These attitudes only cause more discord. Labor is not the problem. Management is not the problem. Employees, white collar and blue collar, management, staff and labor all contribute to low productivity, unsatisfactory job performance and reduced profitability. The "blame" transects the entire corporate structure. In any small, medium or large company, the "blame" for avoidable losses can be distributed equally among the company strata.

It is true that there are measurable differences between specific employees' productivity and efficiency. But the responsibility for conditions that result in inefficiency and production deficits must be shared by all. The time and energy spent on blame-games can be put to much better use and with much more profitable results.

It is difficult for people not to slip into blaming because it is difficult for most people to accept responsibility for the consequences of their own behavior. It is particularly difficult when one's emotions are involved or one's own behavior is threatened with necessary or mandatory change. One's ego is immediately threatened when "blame" is taken as synonymous with "wrong" or "dumb" or "bad."

Part of the problem is cultural. Blaming is deeply imbedded in our American heritage of Puritanism with its strong emphasis on right/wrong, where right equals good and wrong equals bad.

Political parties run their campaigns on blaming the other party for all conceivable ills. Management blames labor and vice versa when a company is in trouble. Parents blame children. Children blame each other. It is more important, culturally, to be "right" than to find out what's wrong.

When children get into trouble over school grades or disruptive, even destructive, behavior, parents get angry and blame the children for not behaving themselves, for causing trouble and upsetting the parents. In order to avoid such distressing incidents in the future, the parents will blame, shame, discipline, punish the children or take them to a counselor.

Any such action appears to be reasonable since, after all, the children are the ones who got into trouble.

Many times, though, parental action is taken not for the sake of the child but for the sake of the parents. More often than not, the parents take action to protect *themselves* from the emotional stress caused by the child's behavior.

After one of these upsetting episodes, each participant tends to withdraw and then sulk in silence, nursing their own feelings of guilt and inadequacy.

It's my fault. I'm a bad kid.

It's my fault. I'm a poor parent.

Each outwardly blames the other and inwardly blames themselves.

The same dynamics apply in marketplace situations. Some important procedure is overlooked and a job has to be done over. The supervisor blames the line staff for carelessness. They blame the supervisor for pressure to raise daily production quotas.

Inwardly, they both suffer feelings of guilt and inadequacy. They blame themselves for not being a better suprevisor or a more reliable worker. Each has difficulty in openly accepting responsibility for their share of the problem.

With an on-the-job training program on human behavior, less time would be wasted on blame-games and more time would go into jointly getting a good job done.

VOC™
+ VOCation

Supervisor / Parent of Business and Industry

by: Bob Nass

Blame Games

Sally! Will you go upstairs and get the scissors?

O.K.

HOME SCENE

— Sally turns and trips over her brothers wagon.

It's your fault because you asked me to go upstairs and brothers fault because his wagon was in the way.

I'll tell brother to keep his things picked up.

Sally! Just follow my instructions and it will come out alright.

I don't agree. But your the boss.

WORK SCENE

OUCH!

— Sally preoccupied with her anger at VOC, pinches her finger. —

SALLY AT THE DISPENSARY

How did you do this?

I didn't do it. VOC had to have his way and I knew it wouldn't work. It's his fault, not mine.

Well, you know how VOC is.

— Critique —

Sally has never learned to be responsible for her behavior.

The mother supports Sally's "blame game" rather than encouraging her to be responsible for her own behavior.

The nurse, perhaps because of her anger towards VOC coupled with her fear of disapproval by Sally, supports Sally's "blame game."

If Sally does not resolve the "blame game" it will interfere with all of her relationships, husband-wife, parent-child, supervisor-co-worker, and deprive her of the rewards of love and achievement.

© 1985 Robert A. Nass

88

DAREDEVIL BEHAVIOR

Everyone needs a strong clear sense of self-identity. It begins developing very early in life and can be well established by puberty. Many family values work for the future benefit of the child. In a family that values honesty, acceptance is based on all members being honest. In a family with a strong work ethic, every family member is expected to contribute to household chores.

A danger lies in acceptance of the person based solely on adoption of those values and rejection of the person for noncompliance.

Children want to be pleasing to their parents. They will spend an unusual amount of energy to accomplish a task if they anticipate a favorable response. They will sometimes take unreasonable risks, even endanger their health, for just a moment of praise. If their untiring efforts bring them a just reward, the tone may then be set for the rest of their lives. If they are disappointed in the parents' acceptance of them, an abrupt change in behavior can occur, especially between puberty and late adolescence.

When children perceive acceptance of their behavior as an acceptance of themselves, the pattern will endure. It can have both positive and negative effects.

Take the case of a child who is continually praised for academic achievement. If this is a family value and that particular accomplishment is recognized as acceptance of the total person, then academic achievement will probably last a lifetime with positive and rewarding effects.

Giving praise in some instances can be injurious to the child's health. When this is done, it is usually for the gratification of the parent and not for the welfare of the child. In the case of a male child, a father may encourage "daredevil" behavior. The child, wanting to please daddy, may take risks that go beyond their capacity to control the situation. If such behavior is positively and continually reinforced, that "cute and playful" daredevil behavior can progress to "reckless" behavior.

Ignoring safety rules is often an outgrowth of just such reinforced parental approval — not buckling car seat belts, traveling too fast on highways, not wearing safety glasses on the job, in addition to taking short cuts in various safety procedures. Such people become reckless in many areas of their lives.

Conversely, after making sustained but unsuccessful efforts to gain the approval of parents, children may give up even trying to win that approval. Behavior may change abruptly.

A young person in a home that dresses in a "preppie" style may begin dressing in a "hippie" or "burnout" style. A young person who had been an "A" student may suddenly be failing most subjects.

In the case of the child who refuses to dress preppie like his brothers and sisters, the message is clear that he doesn't think he measures up and, therefore, sets out in another direction to find approval and acceptance.

The case of an "A" student dropping to a "D" student reveals a youngster who is discouraged. There can be other reasons for such behavior but feelings of nonacceptance are a major cause of nonfunction in youth.

The parents' role in the development of the child is crucial. It goes beyond fulfilling the biological and safety needs. It has to be more sophisticated than the trial and error method. It will take a fearless inventory of the parents' own needs and a clear understanding of their expectations of the child in order to assure that these expectations are for the welfare of the child and not to satisfy some unrealistic needs of the parents.

Is the child's daredevil behavior beneficial to the child or good for the pride of the parent? What affect will parents' acceptance/rejection patterns have on the child's future behavior as an adult?

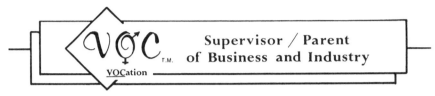

Supervisor / Parent of Business and Industry

$\mathcal{VQC}$ _says:_ Parents often encourage behavior that pleasures them rather than encouraging behavior that benefits the child. What parents encourage often becomes deep rooted in the childs identity.

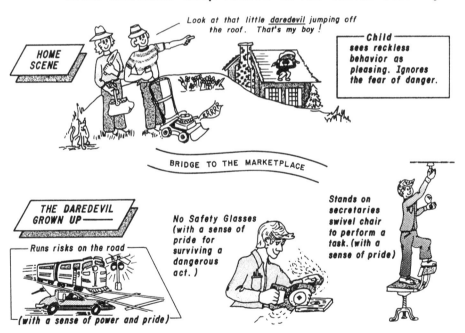

$\mathcal{VQC}$ _says:_ Everyone wants to feel good about themselves. Many take unreasonable risks in order to get that feeling. Others find healthier more fulfilling ways to get self-satisfaction.

DOUBLE MESSAGES

Double messages are usually given when the sender feels pressure from another source and wants to relieve that pressure and "get off the hook." The person usually appears, and actually may be, quite sincere at the moment.

A parent being pestered by a child may make promises to fulfill at some future time. The immediate goal is to stop the pestering. Later on, the promise is broken or the parent tries to substitute the promise made with a less demanding offer.

Some people interject humor in otherwise critical comments. The humor is an avenue of escape for them. If the receiver of the message takes offense, the sender can always say, "I was only kidding.

Sometimes people exaggerate their own capacities to fulfill tasks, agreements or promises in order to enhance their status or self-image. This is not usually done maliciously but the effect on the other person can be just as harmful.

Some messages in response to pressure are deliberate lies.

All the situations have a common characterisitic. The purpose is to relieve the pressure on the message sender who has no regard for the consequences to the other person. The message receiver learns quickly that the sender's word is not trustworthy.

Untrustworthiness has long range consequences. It creates distance between people because of the anger that this type of behavior provokes. It does irreparable harm to the domestic family and can lead to incalculable economic losses in business and industry.

In a domestic vignette, a parent tells the child, as they work together on a project, that he can ask as many questions as he wants. The child accepts the generous invitation and asks his first question. Then he asks a second and a third. Each time the father answers graciously. As the child's questions continue, the father becomes increasingly distracted and impatient. Finally a question provokes an irritable response. "*Now* what do you want?" The child withdraws into silence. Confused and hurt, he thinks to himself, "But you told me I could ask as many questions as I wanted." There follows a painful alienation of two people who love each other.

Many variations of this vignette are played repeatedly in the home, at school, in business and in industry. The results are always the same — feelings of hurt and anger and thoughts of withdrawal or revenge.

Double messages are very difficult to handle. They violate trust. Don't give them.

$\mathcal{VQC}$ says: <u>DOUBLE</u> <u>MESSAGES</u> are difficult to handle. They confuse and frighten people. Try not to give them.

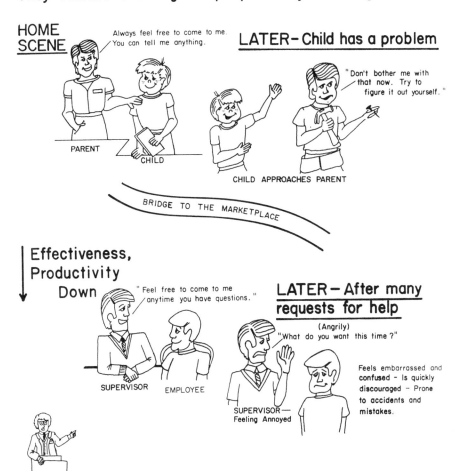

HOME SCENE

Always feel free to come to me. You can tell me anything.

PARENT   CHILD

LATER – Child has a problem

"Don't bother me with that now. Try to figure it out yourself."

CHILD APPROACHES PARENT

BRIDGE TO THE MARKETPLACE

Effectiveness, Productivity Down

"Feel free to come to me anytime you have questions."

SUPERVISOR   EMPLOYEE

LATER – After many requests for help

(Angrily) "What do you want this time?"

SUPERVISOR — Feeling Annoyed

Feels embarrassed and confused – Is quickly discouraged – Prone to accidents and mistakes.

$\mathcal{VQC}$ says: <u>TRUST</u> is the most important element in any good relationship.
Double messages violate trust. Don't give them.

95

BRUSH FIRES

When a relationship seems to be just one hassle after another — certain problems coming up again and again — a sensible person will look for some core *source* of these repeated problems that somehow never stay solved.

Suppose a forest ranger puts out a small brush fire. Then, a few yards away, another ignites. That too he extinguishes. A few minutes later, a third fire has started. The ranger has thoroughly extinguished each separate fire yet new ones continue to start up. There must be some *source* of these brush fires.

He finally discovers a smoldering fire in the trunk of a tree which had been struck by lightning. Each passing breeze was scattering sparks into the brush.

People's lives are something like that. When "brush fires" flare up, over and over, people must look carefully for the source of the problem — the "real" issue that "sparks" repeated "brush fires" in their lives.

Minor fires, unattended, can soon consume the whole forest. Minor problems, unresolved, can soon destroy a whole relationship.

The problem could be a child's behavior, marital conflict, sexual dysfunction, or simply a nagging feeling that something is "missing" in one's life.

The first step toward finding the source of problems is to talk.

VOC _says:_ Multiple problems within a family are like a series of brush fires. that continually require attention or they get bigger. These varied problems usually indicate a deeper rooted personal or family problem. If the deeper rooted problem is not resolved it will continue to ignite new brush fires (areas of concern).

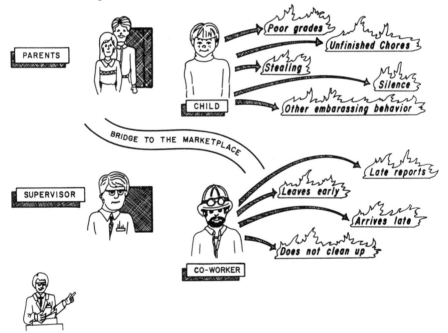

VOC _says:_ If there are multiple problems in your business search for deeper rooted causes by talking with the appropiate people.

THE "IT WASN'T ME, DADDY!" SYNDROME

Some people never do grow up enough to assume responsibility for their own behavior. They may have been so coddled and protected that they don't know how to accept the consequences of their own actions or they may have been so often criticized or ridiculed that they are afraid to accept responsibility. No one enjoys accepting responsibility for wrongdoing.

Some people are so pampered in their developmental stages that they actually feel that others should take care of them, should clean up the messes they make, and correct the mistakes they make.

Others have been so over-criticized for their behavior that to do anything "wrong" seriously threatens their self concept.

Still others will deny responsibility and deliberately shift the blame to someone else, sometimes as a matter of revenge.

A hurt and angry preson may do something that they know will provoke anger. This is their way of getting even. They then deny the provocation so as to seem blameless.

Pampered children are as damaged psychologically as children who are excessively criticized or abused. Both extremes have difficulty with interpersonal relationships.

Parents of pampered children adjust themselves so frequently to meet the needs of the child that it gives the child a distorted perception of the real world. Pampered children act as if, and really believe, rules do not apply to them. They become the takers of the world.

Excessively criticized people deny responsibility for two reasons. First, they may break a rule unwittingly through neglect or absentmindedness. They then fear reprisal and deny their part in the situation in order to prevent the feeling of panic.

Secondly, excessively criticized children feel helpless in negotiating issues effectively. Breaking a rule and then denying any part in it gives them a sense of power. Unfortunately they are unable to sustain any sense of strength or power and so they continually play the "It wasn't me, Daddy!" game.

Neglected, pampered and abused children rarely resolve their historical anger. Breaking rules or disappointing others is a revenge game that seems to relieve that hidden anger. But alas, the anger doesn't remain satisfied. New incidents of provocation will continue to occur.

Dealing with the "It wasn't me, Daddy!" syndrome can be extremely difficult and irritating. If there is only one other person involved, the solution is to offer a clear and simple choice. That person may borrow a tool but if it is not returned, no more tools may be borrowed. The behavior option is then up to the other person.

If more than one person is involved and the offender is not clearly known, responsibility falls, unfairly, on the group as a whole. Those unjustly treated will soon identify and straighten out the actual offender. Everyone remembers a school room experience in which the whole class was punished for the offense of one child who denied guilt.

People also remember how parents handled two children fighting at the dinner table. Both were told to leave the table. They soon agreed between them that decorum is a better choice than hunger.

Eventually, life experiences force people to learn how to accept responsibility for their own behavior.

"IT WASN'T ME DADDY"

HOURS LATER...

— warm milk and dirty glass —

"It wasn't me Daddy!"
(Angry feelings block love)

BRIDGE TO THE MARKETPLACE

— PLEASE —
Everyone wash your own dishes.

MANAGERIAL STAFF MEETING...

Everyone says it wasn't them.

Most of them are angry about it!

Maybe we should close the kitchen!

Maybe we could color code the dishes.

$\mathcal{VOC}$ *says:* Some people have never learned to be responsible for their behavior. Some people disregard rules as a passive expression of their anger.
In either case, those associated with such persons get angry and discouraged. In business and industry anger and discouragement are the major cause of accidents, mistakes and preoccupation thus reducing efficiency and profits.

©1985 Robert A. Nass

SIBLING/COWORKER RIVALRY

Behavior patterns can become well entrenched in childhood and then often last a lifetime. Sibling rivalry can extend itself into adult relationship competitiveness — about sharing friends; being jealous of lovers. It can be seen daily in coworker rivalry.

The mystery surrounding the causes of sibling rivalry has been solved for many years. The older child feels threatened when a newborn enters the family. The older child feels the deprivation of attention from the parents. These feelings are common and often have little to do with the parents' actual love of the older child. Newborns demand and usually get most of the attention.

If the parents are skilled in their role, they can support and nurture the threatened child through his ordeal, thus minimizing the militant attitudes of the siblings. If those feelings are not resolved, they will continue into adulthood and create conflict in friendship, love relationships and in coworker rivalry.

Coworker rivalry is exactly like sibling rivalry with one exception — there is rarely overt physical agitation. All the other "symptoms" are identical. The coworker feels insecure in his role, often feeling inadequate about his own skills and competency and doubtful of his personal equality and worth in the work community.

Feeling inadequate in his role, he sees his only option as reducing the image of his coworkers. This is done by denigrating coworkers to other coworkers or to the boss. He may also withhold information from other coworkers so they will fail in some assignment or at least produce inferior work. In some instances, he may resort to direct sabotage.

Reprimands and other forms of punishment do not help. They only confirm the child's or worker's impression that he is unlikeable, displaced and threatened. The associated message of punishment is that there is something wrong with the person.

The message has to be one of acceptance of the person with the expectation of a change in behavior. This is done by establishing limits of behavior and consequences for breaking those limits.

Options can be suggested. It is then the responsibility of the sibling/coworker to find alternate ways to resolve his feelings.

This at least frees the parent/supervisor from anger. When the parent/supervisor is anger-free, they no longer remain part of the self-fulfilling prophecy of the sibling/coworker — "I don't measure up."

HOME
SCENE

SIBLING/CO-WORKER RIVALRY

*Observes
misdemeanor*

Reports misdemeanor

Sibling rivalry has its roots in the insecurity of the childs perceived status. Unsure of his own performance he downgrades his brothers/sisters performance.

Parents often discourage this behavior by ignoring it or even by scolding the child. The child needs encouragement and support. Parents must learn to be sensitive to the needs of their children.

BRIDGE TO THE MARKETPLACE

WORK
SCENE

Reports misdemeanor
Points out flaws in attitude and performance in order to gain status.

*Observes
misdemeanor*

Co-worker rivalry has its roots in the insecurity of self worth and status.

Management must find a way to improve the feelings of self worth and to encourage co-workers in their own sense of achievements.

VØC *says:* The irony — The report is made to bring favor upon self; A parent or supervisor, feeling inadequate to solve the problem, may resent having the knowledge because they now have the stress of dealing with it or the guilt of not dealing with it.

©1985 Robert A. Nass

THE "WHY SHOULD I?" SYNDROME

When children believe that unfair demands are made of them, they often respond with "Why should I?" A worker who believes he is carrying an unfair share of the workload often responds with "Why should I?"

This message has a two-fold purpose. One is a declaration of discouragement. The manifestation of that discouragement is resistance. Secondly, it is a valid question that asks for and deserves an explanation.

The resistance is not usually a refusal to cooperate but rather an indirect request for a moratorium to discuss the fairness and the terms of the work agreement.

The remark "Why should I?" is usually made when a person feels misused or in a position of disadvantage. This fear is conspicuously observable as irritation or anger. For this reason, the most important part of the message — the valid question "Why?" — is overshadowed by the resistant attitude. The predictable outcome is a struggle for power — a struggle that produces no winners, only losers.

Often the message "Why should I?" is expressed in a more passive way. A child may have been an "A" student through many grades and suddenly does a complete reversal in middle or secondary school. Grades drop, absenteeism increases and general behavior becomes oppositional.

The silent message is "What's the use?" or "Why should I do better?" The youngster has become discouraged. When children have anticipated certain rewards for their efforts and those rewards are not forthcoming, they simply give up and stop trying.

Such behavior is a "yellow flag" — a signal that says "Caution!" — something is wrong. Unfortunately, many parents ignore the danger signs and respond directly to the youngster's negative attitude. Parental power is activated. Punishment is introduced. Privileges are denied. The behavior is attacked without regard to the reason or purpose of that behavior.

At this point, the seriousness of the problem can intensify. Punishment begets anger. Denying previously agreed upon privileges is a breach of trust, creating a spawning ground for fear and anger.

The parent, in an attempt to manipulate the situation, may respond by saying, "If you don't cooperate, then *why should I* do anything for you?" The relationship becomes even more fragile and is in danger of rupturing.

The children, as adults, eventually cross over the "bridge" to the marketplace. The doors of business and the gates of industry open to a stage with a new set. They, as characters, have new roles and new costumes but their behavior patterns remain the same.

The clerk in a store straightens the rack while a coworker takes an extra coffee break. The clerk says to himself, "Why should I care when no one else does?"

The supervisor is conscientious about getting maximum yield while running a smooth operation. Seemingly abruptly, he begins to "look the other way" when there is a critical incident. He says to himself, "If management doesn't care, why should I?" He is clearly disappointed and angry because he thinks management has not been supportive of his efforts.

A worker sees a tool that has been left by someone. He normally would pick it up and return it. This time, he ignores it. The tool will get lost, stolen or damaged.

The problem is ubiquitous and difficult to control. Every critical incident cannot be followed to resolution.

The solution lies in a long term reeducation in the area of human behavior and dignity. People inherently want to be accepted in the community in which they live and work — from the smaller community of their family to the community of business and industry. Children expend a large amount of energy trying to be pleasing. If they are misused, abused or ignored for their efforts, behavior will change abruptly. These behaviors can fluctuate or be continuous and last from cradle to grave.

"Why should I?" is a valid question that requires a sensitive response.

VOC *says:* The *"Why Should I?"* syndrome is an expression of power. It stems from feelings of discouragement, deprivation and anger. When family members have these feelings, they often express them with oppositional behavior.

HOME SCENE

"Please?"   "No! Why should I?"

Parent makes a request.   Child refuses.

───── **PARENT'S OPTIONS** ─────

1. Force the child to do it by using threats.
2. Get a sibling to do it.
3. Don't do it at all.
4. The parents can do it themselves.
5. Try to find the cause of the behavior and negotiate it.

BRIDGE TO THE MARKETPLACE

WORK SCENE

"Please!"   "Why should I? I did my share."

Supervisor makes a request.   Co-worker resists.

───── **SUPERVISOR'S OPTIONS** ─────

1. Force the co-worker to do it by using threats.
2. Get another co-worker to do it.
3. Don't do it at all.
4. The supervisor can do it themselve.
5. Try to find the cause of the resistance and negotiate it.

VOC *says:*

The *"Why Should I?"* syndrome (oppositional behavior) cannot be resolved by using force nor by ignoring it. Try to find the cause of the resistance and negotiate it to mutual satisfaction.

ALCOHOLISM

Alcoholism is an insidious disease because the early symptoms usually go undetected. It is not until the disease is in the advanced stages that the affected person begins to dysfunction in many areas of their life. The earlier the disease is diagnosed and treated, the greater the chance of recovery.

To restate the symptomalogy listed in Part II:

1) Loss of control
2) Chronicity
3) Progression
4) Susceptibility to relapse

Loss of Control — This means simply that there are times when people drink more than they intended to. Loss of control is the inability to predict, once one starts drinking, when one will be able to stop.

Many people are misled by the fact that their loss of control may occur only once in 5, 10 or even 20 drinking occasions. In their own view, they believe that they were controlling their drinking the other 4, 9 or 19 times. That is a false impression. The reality is that an X factor (unknown factor) that triggers loss of control has not been activated on those particular occasions.

This delusion of control is similar to a small child playing a game with a parent. The parent manipulates the game in favor of the child, thus giving the child the impression of victory. The parent is usually subtle but very much in control. Similarly, the X factor in drinking is not precisely predictable but it is very much the factor that controls.

Most people who lose control rationalize it by different types of distorted thinking. "I was just having a good time." "So and so just wouldn't let me leave." "Somebody just kept filling my glass." "It got late before I realized it."

Drinking too much and not realizing it is "loss of control" no matter what excuse is given to deny this most critical of all symptoms of alcoholism.

Usually the loss of control is accompanied by "blackout" — which may go undetected. A blackout is a lapse of memory and should not be confused with "passing out." A person can black-out for a few minutes or for several hours. It can range from a curiosity about what one said or how one acted at a social gathering to awaking in another city without remembering how one got there.

Chronicity — Alcoholism is a chronic disease. One cannot be alcoholic for a week or a month or a year. There is no such thing as an ex-alcoholic. An alcoholic is either actively drinking or sober. There is no conclusive evidence that one can return to social drinking once the major symptoms have been diagnosed. Many have tried; many have failed. Quite often a person may appear to be drinking socially or moderately even for several months or a few years. Remember that the X factor just simply has not yet been activated. Remember also that alcoholism is progressive.

Progressive — The progressiveness of alcoholism means that the drinking will become more frequent, consumption will increase or there will be more of a negative impact when drinking does occur. Sustained drinking, whatever the pattern, leads to deterioration in the major areas of one's life; physically, mentally and emotionally.

112

In the "work ethic" of the United States, alcoholics cling tenaciously to the work record as evidence that alcohol is not a problem. This very attitude often prolongs and intensifies the progression. The family may be fragmented, there may be a drunk driving arrest, but in spite of all the other evidence, the person still says, "I never miss a day's work."

Susceptibility to Relapse — Many people who may recognize that alcohol is causing some problems in their life may interrupt their drinking pattern. Once they feel reassured that the crisis has passed, they believe they can then drink moderately, socially or normally. But they will return to alcoholic drinking, resuming the progression of the disease from the point already reached before they "quit." Each and every drinking episode takes the alcoholic farther into the disease stages. There is no "starting over." Each episode picks up where the last left off and goes on from there.

The lecturer should have expertise in alcoholism as well as family dynamics. The lecture should include the physical and psychological effects on the afflicted person as well as the impact on the entire family structure.

A medium size company of 1,000 employees may have 10 visibly impaired alcoholics. This same company may have as many as 150 who are symptomatic of early or middle stage alcoholism but who may be denying or hiding the problem.

Exposure to lectures and training workshops can encourage those who already suspect a problem to seek help. Those who may need help but simply don't recognize it may be enlightened enough after a lecture to take corrective measures. In either case, management has the benefit of a healthier, more energetic and productive staff.

PARENTING

The goal of parenting is to help children survive and develop toward effective management of their own environment. A generous supply of love and demonstrated affection is a necessary part of children's healthy development.

But love alone does not assure maturity and self-fulfillment in adulthood. It takes skill to raise children to be independent, responsible, even-tempered and reasonably happy, with a good self concept.

Contrary to popular belief in natural instincts, parenting skills are learned, not innate. There is readily available a great deal of misinformation and misinterpreted sound information about parenting. Small wonder that many parents do less than an adequate job.

An example is the common but erroneous equating of discipline with punishment.

Discipline is a necessary part of everyone's life. People feel secure in clusters and so they form communities, large and small. In order for any community to function smoothly, there must be rules. There may be slightly different rules for the community of the home or classroom than for the larger community of a city. Behavior that is incompatible with community rules must be changed or modified if an individual wants to live amicably in a particular community.

Punishment, on the other hand, labels a child or person as "bad" for displaying certain behavior. Punishment is usually a manifestation of the parents own frustration, anger or excessive need for control. Punishment demeans a person, provokes their anger and teaches them to punish others. It does nothing more than that.

When children misbehave or experience frustration and conflict, parents can help them consider options to their conflict. Children can learn that there are consequences to misbehavior without punishing them.

If a child wants to use an adult tool, the child should be instructed in the proper use of the tool and told the consequences of misusing the tool. If then the child does misuse the tool or fails to return it to its proper place, the consequences are denial of the privilege of using adult tools until the child can demonstrate a more responsible attitude. Using consequences to behavior minimizes anger and eliminates the need for punishment.

Another important task for parents is to create an environment for children that is secure enough to allow room for exploring and creating within the limits of their capacities; to aid them in their "limit setting" in time, space and interpersonal relationships.

A playwright once wrote, "The soul of the earth is man and the love of him and we have made of both a desolation."

Parenting is a most responsible job. Parenting skills are necessary to fulfill that responsibility. Lectures, books, support groups and, most of all, training in parenting skills is the best hope we have of reversing that desolation.

HUMAN SEXUALITY

Sex is one of the most intense of all human experiences. Sex can be one of the most pleasurable expressions of a love relationship. Yet many couples are inhibited by their fear and their lack of knowledge and understanding of human sexuality.

Noted researchers in the field of human sexuality claim that in 50% of all couples in the United States, at least one of the partners does not adequately function sexually. With this extremely high incidence of sexual dysfunction, it is important to help people overcome their fears, inhibitions and distorted perceptions about human sexuality.

The lecture should be given by a lecturer certified by the American Association of Sex Educators, Counselors and Therapists. A lecture lasting one and one-half or two hours will enable the audience to exercise their curiosity, give hope to those in need and dispel the many myths that surround this topic.

Important areas to cover in a lecture include the reproductive systems of males and females, the sexual response cycle, male and female genitalia, venereal disease, homosexuality and sexual deviation.

No lecture can be complete without covering sexual dysfunction. In the male, this includes impotence and premature ejaculation, and in the female, vaginismus and orgasmic dysfunction. Dyspareunia (painful coitus) and inhibited sexual desire can be problems for both men and women.

Men and women can be taught to relax with one another and with themselves. They can learn to enjoy playful love and sexual intercourse. They need the opportunity and the courage to attend lectures and training workshops. Some may need family or sex therapy but they will leave the lecture or training workshop encouraged about the possibilities for achieving a happy, satisfying sex life.

Managment, in addition to the humanistic rewards, will reap the profit of a more relaxed energetic and productive employee.

COUPLES GROWING TOGETHER

Couples can have a happy enriched marriage if they expose themselves to education and training. The chances of a good marriage without help are slim. Many experts in the field of marriage therapy estimate the number of happy satisfying marriages to be less than 10%.

In the illustration on page 24, families are placed into six categories:

- Exceptional families   2%
- Healthy families   13%
- Stable families   35%
- Unstable families   35%
- Troubled families   13%
- Impaired families   2%

Couples in any of the lower categories can restructure their marriage and move toward healthiness. There are certain essential components necessary to do this: a never-wavering sense of trustworthiness, a commitment to intimacy through the sharing of feelings, the development of a common value system, the skill of identifying key issues and resolving these issues to mutual satisfaction, an awareness of one's own personal needs, an acknowledgement of one's expectations of the other and cooperation in establishing the limits of those expectations.

Learning how to use those components is extremely difficult for most couples unless they have help. Attending a lecture is a good beginning toward restructuring the marriage. The lectures should include a general overview of the points mentioned above. There should be adequate time allotted for answering specific questions from the audience.

Above all, the lecture is designed to encourage couples to participate in couples growth groups and, in some cases, to direct couples to seek marriage therapy.

COMMUNICATION SKILLS

Good relationships require effective communication. One of the major causes of differences between people is their failure to communicate in a way that promotes understanding and respect for both parties. People usually do not have difficulty hearing the spoken words. It is the distorted perception of those words and the hidden attitudes underlying the spoken word that cause conflict. The second major cause of misunderstanding is the mental-emotional condition of one or both parties at the time of the conversation.

People usually communicate on three levels. Level 1 is informative and is presented in a non-involved objective manner. "Your friend John called at 1 o'clock and wants you to call him back." "Hello! How are you today?" "How is your car running?" "I need directions. Can you help me?"

Level 2 is more complex and addresses issues that impact emotionally on either party. These are issues that have both an intellectual solution and a need for emotional resolution. What causes differences or conflict in Level 2 is that people communicate predominantly from either an intellectual perspective or a predominantly emotional perspective. Effective communications require clear expression and a balance of both thoughts (intellect) and feelings.

A parent may have some anxiety about a task that their spouse or child is obligated to complete. The parent may offer suggestions or encouragement about completing on time but without sharing the feelings (anxiety) behind the prodding. The spouse, or child, insensitive to the anxiety, continues to delay the task. The anxiety level of the parent rises. They may become angry or tearful or display other strong emotions.

Step 1 — Anxious parent — offers intellectual advice, suppresses anxiety.

Step 2 — Spouse or child — explains why task is not urgent or simply ignores anxious parent.

Step 3 — Anxious parent — anxiety elevates and may manifest itself in an outburst of anger or tears.

The third step could have been avoided if the anxious parent had shared their thoughts and feelings on the issue. The appropriate sharing of thoughts and feelings is Level 3.

It is this latter style that brings people closer together in a more intimate and cooperative way. Both parties can reach a practical (intellectual) solution to any problem while sharing an understanding of feelings, each of the other.

Mutual respect and mutual cooperation are requisites for healthy and effective negotiation. This is true of parent-child, husband-wife, and management-staff relationships.

One absolute taboo when using Level 2 or 3 communications is no alcohol. Level 1 communication can be used under the influence of alcohol without damage to anyone. But when communication is on Level 2 or 3, even a single glass of wine distorts the perception. Many a promise has been made over a single drink only to be broken or regretted when the effect of the small amount of alcohol wears off.

People can save themselves a lot of heartache if they adopt a rule of no alcohol when discussing issues where there is emotional involvement. In general, people have no concept of the effect on the emotions and the distortion of perceptions caused by even a single drink of alcohol, beer or wine. The automobile industry and federal safety agencies have measured alcohol effect on visual-motor coordination. They have concluded that even a single drink (in any form) has a negative effect. The same is true of the mental-emotional coordination.

Most people will have a difficult time accepting this because a drink helps them relax (reduces anxiety) and they have a sense that they do better with a small amount of alcohol. Precisely the point. "Relaxed" when a decision or promise is made, then left with the task of following through on the decision or promise when anxiety has returned to the normally higher level.

A lecture on communications *must* include the above.

UNDERSTANDING AND COPING WITH ANGER

If there are to be peaceful, loving and prosperous families, if there are to be cooperative and profitable businesses, if nations hope to live in peace, people will have to reduce their fear and cope more effectively with that devastating manifestation of fear — anger.

The lecture "Understanding and Coping with Anger" will provide new insights for people through an awareness of the causes of anger and offer appropriate options to anger.

This lecture can be given comfortably to between 100 and 150 people. Limiting the size to this number makes it more manageable for the lecturer in two areas.

- A "fish bowl" demonstration using 6-10 volunteers is effective in showing how people can minimize anger through effective problem solving and understanding the causes of their anger.

- There can be greater participation and interaction to the question, answer and discussion at the end of the lecture.

It is necessary for the lecturer to be well versed in the correlation between fear and anger, clearly demonstrated with real life illustrations. Adequate time and appropriate illustrations should be given to the various styles that people use in expressing their anger.

The above topics are a must but the lecturer is not limited to their expression. Physiological comparisons of fear and anger may be discussed. Some lecturers may choose to give a brief handout test on how individuals presently express their anger in trying situations.

The training sessions on both "Parenting" and "Couples Growing Together" have a section on anger resolution so the audience will have a chance to experience in controlled conditions what they learn in the lecture.

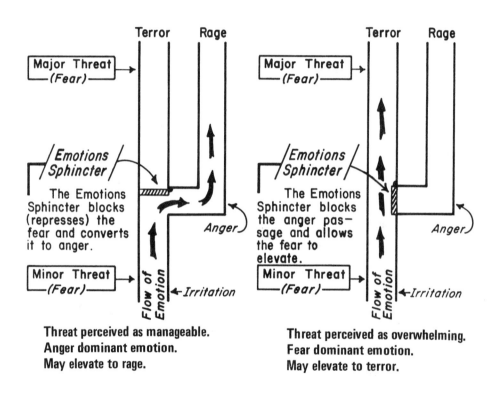

Threat perceived as manageable.
Anger dominant emotion.
May elevate to rage.

Threat perceived as overwhelming.
Fear dominant emotion.
May elevate to terror.

Fear is the alarm system to impending threat. Anger is the protective mechanism. If danger is perceived to be manageable, anger will elevate from irritation to rage, depending on how much energy the person thinks is needed to control the impending threat.

If the person, at any point, perceives the threat as overwhelming, the anger will revert back to the continuuum of fear to terror and the person will attempt to withdraw.

PARENTING SKILLS

The home is the basic "training site" for the people who eventually arrive at the work site. Parents are the primary trainers in early rearing. The child then has other trainers who also are products of their own particular training sites and parent trainers. Simply put, everyone who works was trained in interpersonal relationships by domestic trainers called parents.

Parents have an important impact on the efficient functioning of employees in business and industry. Consequently business and industry have a vested interest in helping parents become good at parenting.

Poor parenting produces poor workers. Poor workers waste time, have accidents, make mistakes and do damage that directly affects a company's productivity and profitability.

Parenting training requires approximately 16 hours. A manageable group should be limited to approximately 20 participants. It should be set up group style with chairs in a circle. This affords better interaction and better eye contact.

Eight topics are included in this 16 hour period. Approximately 2 hours is allotted to each topic. Ideally, a separate topic should be discussed each week for 8 weeks. This allows time to digest each topic and to apply it before moving on to the next topic. Other variations are acceptable such as 4 hours of group sessions covering two topics at a time and given on 4 successive Saturdays.

The 8 topics included in the training are:

1) *Trust* — The most basic and important component of good relationships.

2) *Expectations and Limit Setting* — Children must have a clear understanding of what you expect from them. As much as children constantly "test" the stated limits, they actually become frightened if they are not sure of what the limits actually are.

3) *Discipline vs. Punishment* — Discipline teaches responsibility. Punishment provokes anger.

4) *Communications* — Gives understanding. Paraphrase as many times as it takes to understand.

5) *Problem-solving by Negotiation* — Helps children and parents to consider options. Negotiation brings mutual acceptance.

6) *Effective Anger Resolution* — Unresolved anger blocks love and divides families.

7) *The Message Behind the Behavior* — Children are not sophisticated enough to communicate verbally, so they "act out" the message — which is often misinterpreted by adults. The result is family fragmentation.

8) *Mutual Respect and Freedom to be Creative* — Enhances the self worth of the child and promotes the courage to try.

HUMAN SEXUALITY

Human sexuality is a very important aspect of a person's life. Unfortunately, many individuals and couples suffer from feelings of inadequacy and all too often this leads to sexual dysfunction. Proper education, training and therapy can produce a healthier attitude along with a more pleasurable sex life.

Joe and his wife were recently divorced after 20 years of marriage. Shorty thereafter, Joe began therapy for reasons other than sexual problems. He recalled his marital history. Sex was frequent early in the marriage but love-making gradually decreased in frequency until it became nonexistent. Joe had always had a problem with premature ejaculation. He sometimes ejaculated prior to intromission or within seconds after entering. When this happened, he would apologize to his wife. She would say, "That's okay" and they would both roll over and go to sleep.

Sex was not their only problem but it did impact upon the other areas of their life and it was a major contributor to their separation. After entering therapy, Joe corrected his problems and was able to control his ejaculation for several minutes after intromission.

This and various other types of sexual dysfunction are not uncommon and can cause major discord between couples, with damaging effects on family life.

Dysfunction Terminology:

Premature Ejaculation — Ejaculation prior to, upon, or within seconds after intromission.

Impotence — The inability to have penile erection or to maintain erection for a sufficient amount of time to have sexual intercourse.

Dyspareunia — Painful sexual intercourse.

Vaginismus — Intense muscle spasms with the vagina that prevent penetration of the penis into the vagina.

Orgastic Dysfunction — The inability for the female to enter the orgasmic phase.

Sex is a pleasurable and intense experience. It is a marvelous expression of love between two people. It generates love feelings. Love manifests in happiness and tenderness and — above all, love is generous.

Loving, happy, generous people are productive people.

SAMPLE MODEL FOR
HUMAN SEXUALITY WORKSHOP

I. OVERVIEW AND GENERAL COMMENTS

II. GENERAL INFORMATION
    A. Understanding Terms
    B. Human Sexual Response
    C. Reproductive System — Male
    D. Reproductive System — Female

III. HUMAN SEXUAL INADEQUACY
    A. Female
        1. Orgasmic Dysfunction
        2. Vaginismus
        3. Dyspareunia
    B. Male
        1. Premature Ejaculation
        2. Primary and Secondary Impotence
        3. Retarded Ejaculation

IV. GROUP DISCUSSION

ALCOHOLISM

Within the past decade, with increased awareness of the complexity of human behavior, there has been an increased demand and desirability for new approaches in helping troubled members of the community.

The purpose of this workshop is to create awareness of and insight into the dynamics of the alcoholic family.

Understanding alcoholism has been slow and difficult for many employers and professionals and as a consequence, we have failed too often to effectively help its victims.

Fear pervades every aspect of alcoholic families' lives — fear of dependence, fear of failure, fear of intimate relationships, fear of parent role, fear of responsibility — all of which develops into a generalized fear that these separate "threats" cannot be coped with and life will never be structured, stable and comfortable.

Alcoholics, like everyone else, unconsciously disguise internal fears into behavior that is perceived externally by others as anger. It may take the form of irritability, inconsistency, exaggerated reactions to minor normal incidents, abuse, destruction and even criminal behavior.

This workshop will provide participants with a working knowledge of the development of unhealthy need fulfillment in relationships such as those in an alcoholic family, how family members

133

themselves contribute to their own destructiveness and how employers as well as therapists, physicians, court and police personnel, and even the community at large, contribute to the overall problem and in many ways participate in the acting out behavior of the alcoholic.

GOALS AND OBJECTIVES

The ultimate goal of all training activities is to provide more effective service to clients. A more specific goal is to provide a training experience that will create insight into the dynamics of the alcoholic family so that employers, employees and family members can anticipate response behavior and thus minimize conflict and facilitate effective problem-solving processes.

The training program is designed to achieve the following objectives:

- Sensitize staff and family members to the complex need fulfillment that motivates behavior.
- Increase staff's ability to assess clearly and accurately the extent of the employee's needs.
- Increase knowledge of alcoholism.
- Increase awareness of workplace behavior as an integral extension of the domestic family's behavior.
- Increase awareness of community resources available to the employee.
- Improve understanding of delinquent behavior as a response to family difficulties.
- Improve understanding of the non-alcoholic spouse's own needs in supporting the alcoholic's drinking and destructive behavior.
- Provide insight into the alcoholic's purpose in both alcoholic and deviant behavior.

The objectives of the training will be achieved through the provision of lecture, film, demonstration, and experiential opportunities in the following areas of concentration:

1. Crisis intervention
2. Disease concept of alcoholism
3. Role purpose of family members
4. Self-exploration of relationships
5. Family development.

SAMPLE MODEL FOR "ALCOHOLISM" WORKSHOP

TOPIC	CATEGORY	SKILLS AND KNOWLEDGE	FORMAT
1. Family Development	Pre-marriage Attraction	Knowledge of Family Dynamics	Didactic Presentation
	Marital Development	Knowledge of Emotional Need Ful-fillment	Case examples
	Marital Conflict	Family Assessment Skills	Group Participation
		Behavioral Observation Skills	Group Discussion
			Question and Answer
2. Alcoholism	Disease Concept	Knowledge of Alcoholism	Didactic Presentation
	The Family Roles	Skill of Early Identification	Film
	Male Parent	Knowledge of Cause and Effect	Case Examples
	Female Parent	Understand Role Development	Group Discussion
	Family Violence	Skill in Assessing Marital and Child	Question and Answer
	Sexuality	Knowledge of Sexual Abuse and Dysfunction	
3. Recap			Discussion - Review
4. Family Treatment	Self Help Organizations	Skill in Assessing Needs	Lecture
	Professional-Private-Public Agencies	Knowledge of "Where To Turn" for Referral	Pamphlets
5. Case Presentation	Role Play	Role Identity	Experiential Demon-stration
		Skill in Problem Identification	Audience Participation as Characters
		Skill in Problem Solving	Group Discussion
			Question and Answer
6. Summary and Wrap-Up	All of the Above	Same as Above	Group Discussion
			Question and Answer

COUPLES GROWING TOGETHER

The training workshop on Couples Growing Together gives participants several benefits. It will help them identify issues that cause conflict in their marriage. It will teach them a new style of communication and give them a chance to experience a dialogue that helps resolve conflict to mutual satisfaction. They will have the advantage of feedback from other participants. They will learn to identify their feelings and gain a new pleasurable experience in sharing feelings.

There are three necessary components to good training workshops. Developing trust in a relationship as part of one's value system. Developing a communication system that reduces conflict and anxiety. Developing an awareness and sensitivity to the needs and expectations, including limit setting, of the couple.

Trust — It is not possible to have a good relationship without trust. You can have a bad relationship without trust but not a good one.

Trust simply means that you keep your word. You keep your promises. Many married couples limit trust to sexual loyalty without regard to other areas in their life. This can be an absurd limitation. If one cannot trust that a spouse will be home at an agreed upon time, how difficult it must be to believe the excuse for not keeping the agreement.

Trust, like the famous soap, has to be 99 44/100 pure. There is no such thing as being trustworthy most of the time. Trust is too fragile and important. If your doctor keep his appointments most of the time but not all the time (99 44/100), there would be anxiety for the patients every time they set out to go to the office. If the train came most of the time but not all of the time, the commuters would have anxiety every time they used the train. If they commuted every day, they would have anxiety every day. There is that same correlation in marriage. The couple whose trust level is less than 99 44/100 is an anxious couple. Anxiety is fear. Fear converts to anger and anger blocks love.

In the training workshop, couples can talk freely to each other about areas that frighten and anger them when there is a breach of trust. Together they can grow into a trustworthy couple and release the anger that blocks their love.

Communications — Many couples give incomplete or warped messages when they talk about issues of concern. They are also more apt to refer to events without mention or regard to their feelings about those events.

To illustrate, a man recently declared to his wife that he had planned to meet an old friend for a "night on the town" and asked if that was okay. His wife had some anxiety and was angered by his solo activity but responded by saying, "That's fine!" She said it with an angry expression. She did not really mean that it was fine nor did she talk about how she really felt about it. The husband was also relieved that she did not talk about her feelings. He sensed her anger but his eagerness to meet his friend took top priority and he was sure he could calm her down later.

The wife soon reopened the conversation. She started by talking about chores that had not been completed. She also proposed an overdue visit to a relative in place of his meeting his friend. There ensued a battle of wits and a struggle for power. They both spent a great deal of energy talking about the event but did not share their feelings about the event or about each other.

138

Early training by unskilled trainers (parents and other adults) causes this difficulty in expressing honest and direct feelings. These early trainers are usually sincere and almost always love their children and want the best for their children. They are simply unskilled and trained poorly, albeit unwittingly. A parent is often overheard saying to the child, "Don't feel that way." When someone is sad, another will say, "Cheer up!" (change that feeling; it's bad.) When they become too exuberant, someone will say, "Calm down. Don't get so hysterical." (the feeling is too extreme; change it.) Don't be mad, don't be silly, don't be hurt, don't be disappointed. Change those feelings, change those feelings.

The message is clearly understood. It is bad or wrong to offer direct and honest expression of one's feelings. Soon children begin to think whether or not they should express the feeling. Then they begin to suppress and deny their feelings. Hence the classic response to "How do you feel" — "I don't know."

There are two basic options. Learn to share feelings or live in a distant marriage. It's that simple.

Needs and Expectations — People seldom take a conscious and deliberate inventory of their needs and expectations. The expectations include "limit setting." It is or it is not alright to have a night out with the boys. If it is alright, are there clear and agreed upon activities?

In a marriage, there are expectations that directly affect the needs of the spouse. Many needs on the other hand have little impact upon other people. The need for affection, for instance, correlates with an expectation for the spouse to be affectionate. If affection is denied, there is a problem.

The need for financial stability correlates with the expectation that the spouse be financially responsible. If they are not, there will be a problem.

A need for sharing feeling will be frustrated if feelings are not shared.

A need for adventure, on the other hand, may not carry any

more of an expectation than patience from the spouse. The adventurous need may be fulfilled by a solo activity such as climbing a mountain or walking part of the Appalachian Trail.

In expressing needs, couples must be very specific. General requests can bring poor results. Simply stating that they want more affection doesn't help the spouse who may think that they are very affectionate already. An argument goes on for years in the style of the schoolyard debate — "No, you're not." "Yes, I am." A specific request should be simple and measurable. "I need a hug." "Let's hold each other nightly before we go to sleep."

Financial stability and responsibility are established by setting mutually agreed upon limits on the budget. General statements are ineffective. "Don't spend too much" is too general and too vague and will cause anxiety in both parties. One worrying about how much to spend and the other worrying about how much will be spent. Anxiety always interferes with the expression of love.

Couples Growing Together training is necessary if couples are to learn how to be trustworthy, develop a good system of communication and develop an intimacy through the sharing of feelings in order to get their needs met. If their needs are not met, they will not be mentally alert enough to maximize their achievements in the marketplace.

Format:	Group style — Chairs in circular arrangement
	Maximum of 12 couples (24 people)
Duration:	Approximately 14 hours.
	Variations: 1) Weekend retreat
	2) Successive Saturdays
	3) Weekly 2-hour sessions

PEER SUPPORT GROUP (PSG)

Purpose: (To be read at the start of each session)

The primary purpose of the Peer Support Group (PSG) is to create a supportive climate for supervisors and managers. It is designed to promote an attitude of cooperation, responsibility and unity within the business/industrial family.

It has the purpose of teaching problem-solving techniques; facilitating the sharing of on-the-job personal experiences; creating a new awareness and understanding of counterproductive behavior.

Objectives: (To be read at the start of each session)

1)   Create a relationship within the business/industrial family that will support organizational goals while encouraging personal achievement.

2)   Foster the type of relationship between management and staff that promotes cooperation, confidence, responsibility and mutual growth of both the organization and of each employee.

Rules and Guidelines:

1)   *Meet weekly* for approximately 1-1/4 hours.

2)   *Participants must be prompt.* At least a full hour of sharing is necessary for optimum results. Approximately 15 minutes of each session will be spent reviewing the objective and generally

reducing the anxiety level. Tardiness by members may represent an acting out of their own anxiety or it may be symptomatic of their oppositional behavior, designed to disrupt the effectiveness of the group.

Such behavior should be discussed within the group because it is this very behavior that is so counter-productive to any organization.

3) *Consistent Attendance.* Loyalty to the group is essential in attaining the objectives. The consistency of the group is interrupted when someone misses a session. It is unrealistic to deny that members will go on vacation, be sick, take a personal day or have emergencies in their department. High level anxiety members or oppositional members may frequently schedule their personal days on the PSG meeting day. "Emergencies" in their department may be exaggerated or even manufactured. If these are even suspected by other group members, it should be discussed openly within the group setting and with the "suspected" party present.

Maligning another person "behind their back" without attempts to resolve the issue is, to repeat, counter-productive to the mission of the group.

4) *Avoid technical problems.* Discuss only interpersonal behavior problems.

5) *Avoid criticism.* Group members are to work toward the common objectives. This is best done by sharing experiences. One supervisor may think that another is foolish for not addressing a particular issue with an employee or may criticize the manner in which it is done. To confront the supervisor with such a remark would only make the other person defensive and the reaction would be rationalization, anger or withdrawal; also counter-productive.

A more effective, productive and more sensitive approach is to share experiences. One supervisor might respond, "You know, Sam, I know how you feel. I had a guy working for me that always knew just how far he could go and it used to frustrate me and make me angry. But I was actually afraid to say anything because he always seemed to outwit me by having reasonable excuses. I would think of him when I first got up in the morning and he was the last thing I thought of at night. It was an awful feeling and an awful experience."

No solution was actually suggested at that moment. There was only a sharing of experience and an identity of feelings. Other supervisors may, at this time, share other similar experiences.

After this type of sharing and interaction, someone or perhaps the leader may invite comments in order to effect a collective group decision on how to approach the troublesome employee and to negotiate a mutually satisfying solution.

6) *Confidentiality*. Confidentiality should be honored by all group members.

7) *There should be no confronting*. The group sessions should be kept as non-threatening as possible in order to facilitate the attitude of support.

Prerequisites:

1) *Composition*. The size of the PSG should be 6-10 participants including a designated group leader.

A small company with less than six supervisors can use all available supervisors and managers and include company officers.

2) *Training*.

a) *Leaders* for the PSG are best trained off-site in a concentrated block of time (1 week.)

Included in that training will be the four main areas of people problems: Alcoholism, Parenting, Human Sexuality and Couples Growing Together. Understanding and coping with anger as well as communication skills are included in both the Parenting and the Couples Growing Together workshops.

Ten hours of training will be experiential. Leader-trainees will observe, share thoughts and feelings and resolve critical incidents in a group setting.

b) *Non-leaders* supervisors must have attended a training

course in either Parenting or Couples Growing Together prior to their first PSG session. Completion of all lectures and training in the remaining workshops can be completed concurrently with the weekly PSG sessions.

WHAT TO EXPECT

Each group session should begin with a reading of the purpose and objectives by the leader. This reinforces a need for commitment toward common goals and objectives.

In the beginning, there may be some silliness, some joking and even some sarcasm. This behavior is a manifestation of the anxiety that the participants are experiencing. It is new to them and it may be frightening. It is the leader's task to help them through their anxieties and to assure them of the long term positive benefits. They should also be assured that they cannot fail the group; there are no grades for performance. They can only enhance their awareness, confidence and effectiveness as a supervisor of people.

The leader may want to introduce a warm-up exercise to help break the ice. One such exercise might be to pass out 3x5 cards and ask each participant to write down two strong points and two weak points about themselves. The leader does the same. After about 5 minutes, the leader then shares his own strengths and weaknesses with the group and invites comment. The group can ask questions until the questions are exhausted. Then someone else is asked to voluntarily share what they have written and to invite comment.

At any time, a participant may refuse to answer any questions. Keep in mind that it is a non-confronting group. No one enjoys feeling trapped. No one likes to be criticized.

When the warm-up exercise is complete, the leader can explain the procedure which the group will follow in successive sessions. It might be as follows:

1) Open with reading of the purpose and objectives. This is important for the solidarity of the group. It helps to create an *exprit de corps*. It is based on the same principles as the salute to the flag, repeating a religious creed or saying the Boy Scout oath.

2) An invitation for personal comments, the nature of which may interfere with that person's full attention to group. It could be a domestic concern, an attitude or even a discomfort related to the group arrangement.

3) An invitation to voluntarily discuss a recent "critical incident." The incident might be misuse of equipment or product by an employee, a subordinate's remark or any of a variety of behavioral problems. A "critical incident" may also be of a positive nature such as an employee's suggestion on how to improve a particular product or production procedure.

4) Each session will have assigned a supervisor to present an appraisal of one of the employees in his particular department. Each group can decide on the format of presentation or it can be uniform throughout the company. A model format may include:

   a) Background information such as longevity with the the company, time in grade, attendance records and other identifying remarks.

   b) Accident and safety record.

   c) Outstanding achievements.

   d) Comments on motivation, attitude and cooperativeness.

   e) Chief complaints of that employee.

   f) Particular problems that impact upon coworkers.

   g) How this employee impacts upon the supervisor.

   h) What feelings does the supervisor have toward this employee?

   i) Supervisor's posture and attitude and method or style

146

in dealing with this employee.

Comments or questions may be offered as the presentation progresses or they may be held until the end. The presenter's comfort level should be a determining factor. All of this is followed by open discussion.

The PSG will have a positive effect on its participants. Some will be affected more rapidly than others. The more involved they become in sharing their feelings, the more rapidly they will progress in enhancing their interpersonal relationship skills. Those who are more silent may not progress as rapidly but they also will reap the benefits if they continue regular attendance.

The PSG will create a sense of unity, support, cooperation and, in general terms, an *esprit de corps* rarely experienced in the business/industrial complex. Personally the PSG will enhance the skill of problem-solving and offer opportunities to develop self-confidence in interacting with people at all levels.

The PSG will be an encouraging force in direct and more immediate resolution of personnel problems.